Burford Ontario Book 1 in Colour Photos, Saving Our History One Photo at a Time

Photography
by Barbara Raué
2017

Series Name:
Cruising Ontario

Book 182: Burford Book 1

Cover photo: 155 King Street, Page 38

Series Name: Cruising Ontario
Saving Our History One Photo at a Time
in colour photos

Books Available in Alphabetical Order:
Aberfoyle, Acton, Alton, Amherstburg, Ancaster, Arthur, Aylmer, Ayr, Bloomingdale, Brantford, Burlington, Caledon, Caledonia, Cambridge, Clifford, Conestogo, Delhi, Dorchester to Aylmer, Drayton, Drumbo, Dundas, Eden Mills, Elmira, Elora, Essex, Fergus, Guelph, Hagersville, Hamilton, Hanover, Harriston, Hespeler, Jarvis, Kingston, Kingsville, Kitchener, Linwood, Listowel, London, Lucknow, Mono, Mount Forest, Neustadt, New Hamburg, Niagara-on-the-Lake, Oakville, Orangeville, Orillia, Owen Sound, Palmerston, Peterborough, Petrolia, Port Elgin, Preston, Rockwood, Sarnia, Seaforth, Sheffield, Shelburne, Simcoe, Southampton, St. Jacobs, St. Marys, St. Thomas, Stoney Creek, Stratford, Thamesford, Tillsonburg, Waterdown, Waterford, Waterloo, Welland, Wellesley, Windsor, Wingham, Woodstock

Book 157: Brockville
Book 158: Merrickville
Book 159: Smiths Falls
Book 160: Portland, Newboro
Book 161: Westport & Area
Book 162: Perth
Book 163-166: Belleville
Book 167-168: Port Colborne
Book 169: Erin in Colour
Book 170: Goderich in Colour
Book 171: Sault Ste. Marie
Book 172: Lake Superior
Book 173-176: Thunder Bay
Book 177-179: Paris

Book 180-181: St. George
Book 182-183: Burford

Other Books by Barbara Raue

Coins of Gold

Arrows, Indians and Love

The Life and Times of Barbara
Volume 1: Inventions That Have Enhanced My Life
Volume 2: Entertainment That I Have Enjoyed
Volume 3: East Coast Trips
Volume 4: Olympics Have Always Intrigued Me
Volume 5: Wonders of the World
Volume 6: Caribbean Cruises We Have Enjoyed
Volume 7: Animals
Volume 8: Storms and Other Major Disasters in My Lifetime
Volume 9: Wars, Terrorist Attacks and Major Disasters

The Cromwell Family Book

Laura Secord Discovered

Daddy Where Are You?

Montana Series
Book 1: Montana Dream
Book 2: Life on the Montana Frontier
Book 3: Montana to Boston and Back
Book 4: Montana Sons Go to War
Book 5: Montana Sons Return From War

Visit Barbara's website to view all of her books
http://barbararaue.ca

Table of Contents

Highway 53	Page 6
West Quarter Townline Road	Page 11
Minshall Drive	Page 13
King Street	Page 16
Maple Avenue North	Page 46
Sixth Concession Road	Page 49
Saint William Street	Page 50
Seventh Concession Road	Page 51
Dufferin Street	Page 52
Jarvis Street	Page 55
John Street	Page 56
Potter Drive	Page 57
Alexander Street	Page 58
Architectural Terms	Page 61
Building Styles	Page 65

Burford is in the County of Brant and is located eight kilometers west of the City of Brantford along Highway 53, and seventy kilometers east of London.

In 1793 Lieutenant-Governor Simcoe granted to Abraham Dayton the entire Township of Burford. Dayton was a native of Milford, Connecticut. The township was to become the "new Jerusalem" for a religious sect with which he was affiliated. Dayton broke his ties with the sect and settled just west of the present village of Burford. He was responsible for bringing several families into the township and by the spring of 1797 the new settlement consisted of twenty-one families. Abraham Dayton died March 1, 1797 after a prolonged illness. Abigail Dayton, Abraham's widow, later married Colonel Joel Stone and moved to Gananoque where she lived until her death in 1843 at the age of 93. The Dayton's only child, Abiah, was the wife of Benajah Mallory and she and her husband followed her parents into this township. Benajah Mallory became a man of considerable influence and by 1805 was elected Member of the Legislative Assembly of Upper Canada representing Norfolk, Oxford, and Middlesex. In June 1812, war was declared against Upper Canada by the United States. During the course of the war, Mallory accepted a commission in the U.S. forces and was considered a traitor back home. Benajah Mallory became outlawed and his land was forfeited to the Crown.

John Yeigh, his wife Mary and their children Jacob, John Junior, Adam, Henry and Eva arrived in Burford from Pennsylvania by covered wagon in June 1800. The family cleared land, farmed and established the first pottery in the Burford area. Jacob and Adam distinguished themselves in the War of 1812 and were also active participants in the 1837 Rebellion.

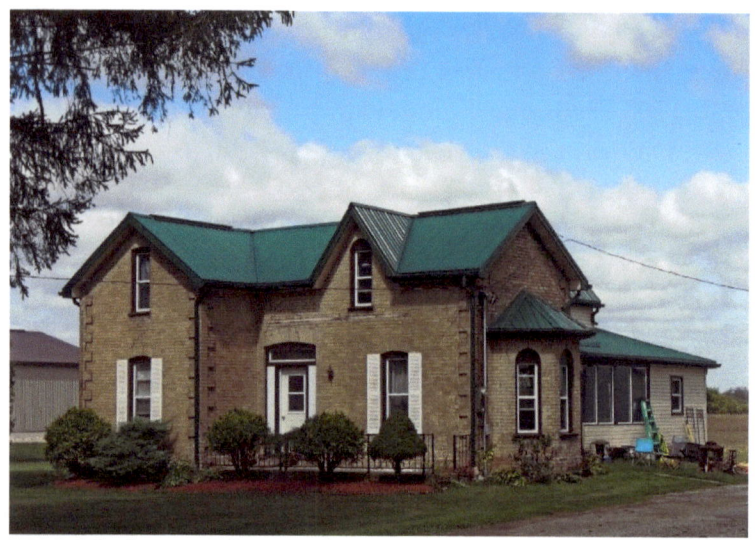
1319 Highway 53 – Gothic, corner quoins, bay window

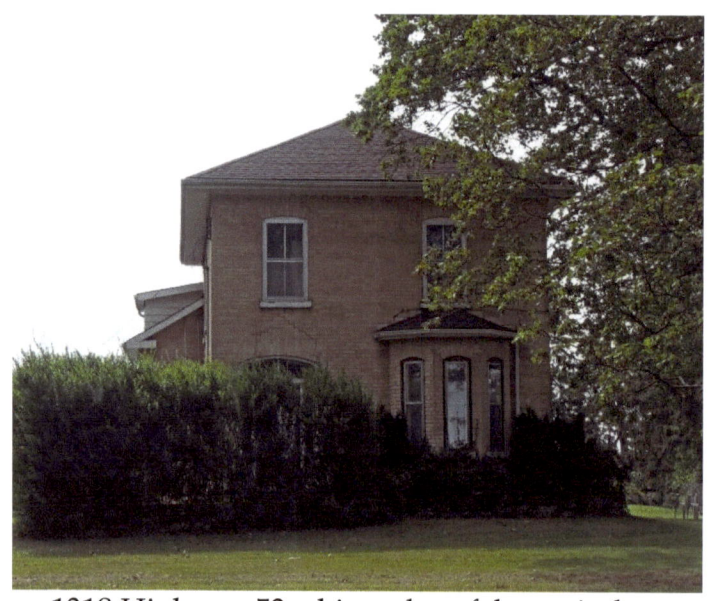
1318 Highway 53 – hipped roof, bay window

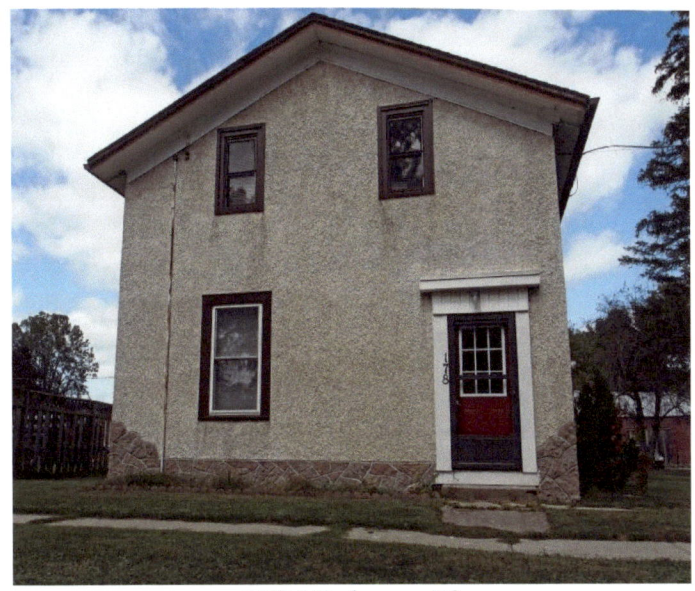

178 Highway 53

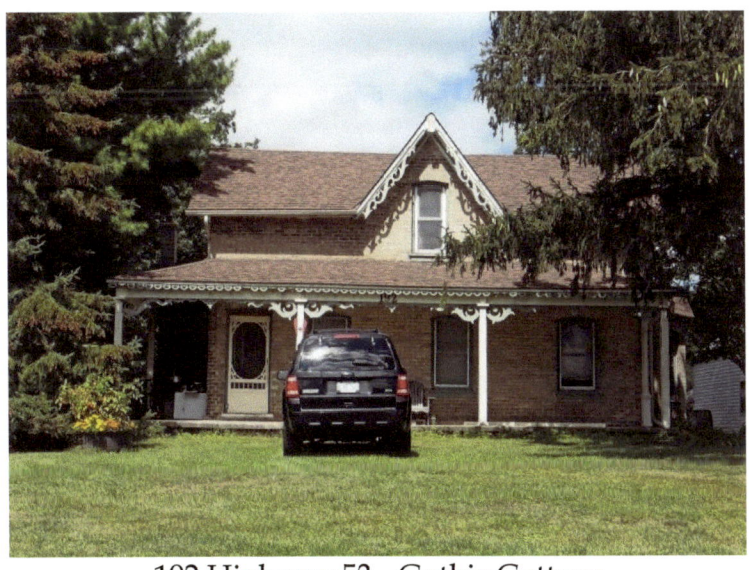

192 Highway 53 - Gothic Cottage

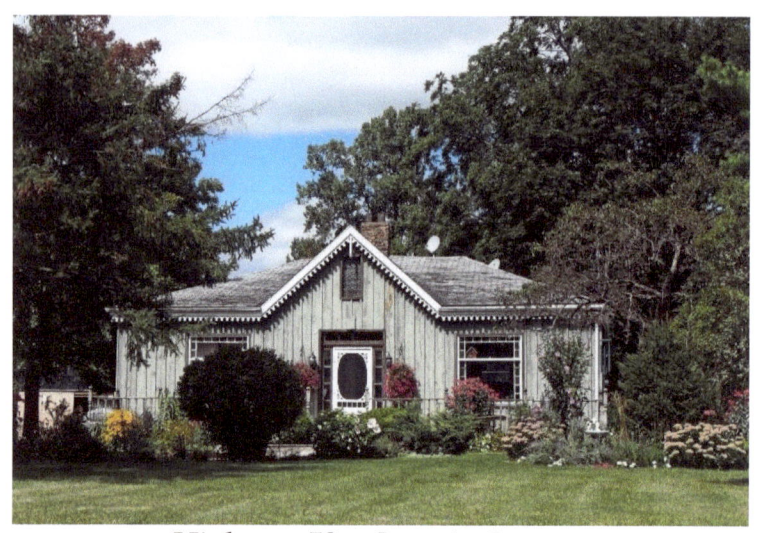

Highway 53 – Ontario Cottage

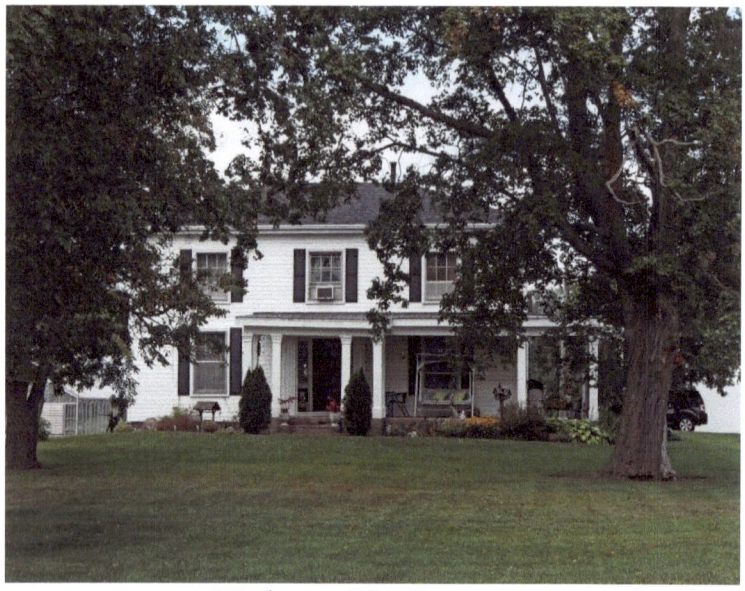

Highway 53 - Georgian

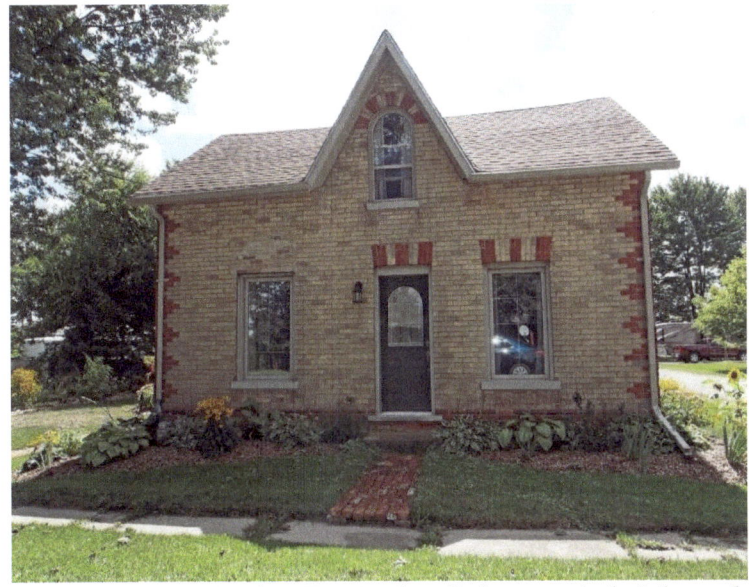

Highway 53 – Gothic Revival – dichromatic brickwork

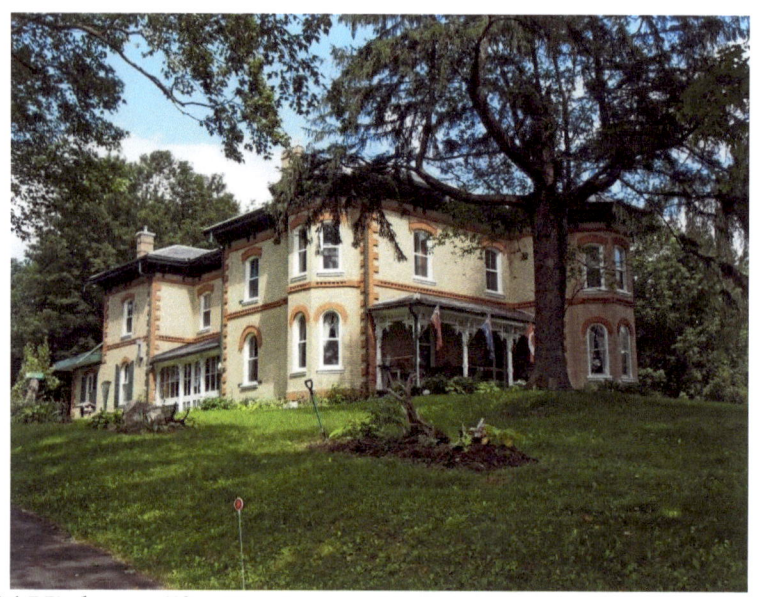

306 Highway 53 – Farrington House – 1883 – built by James Farrington – Italianate style with buff brick, decorative red stringcourse and arches over the Roman style windows. The original front and side porches have gingerbread trim. James Farrington traveled to California during the gold rush and was involved in many successful business enterprises including ranching, gold and silver mining and high plains freighting.

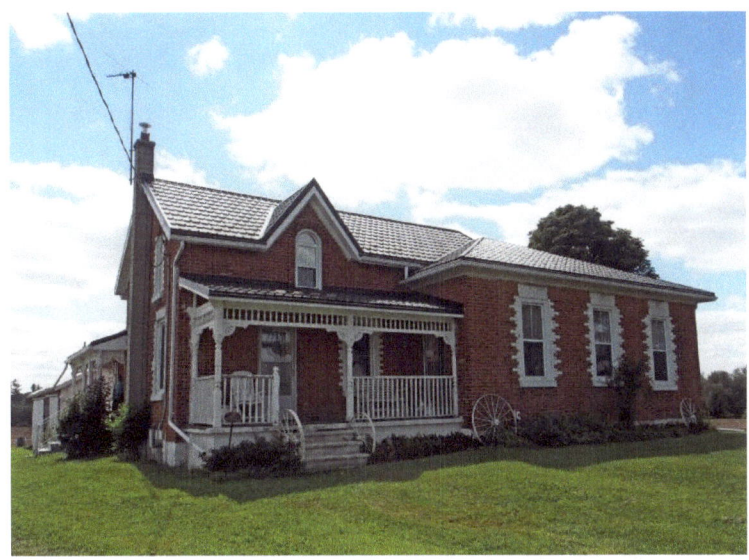

378 West Quarter Townline Road – Heritage Property – This house has Roman influenced windows with alternating brick to simulate quoining and geometric shapes such as diamonds in the apex of the gable ends. It has three gable ends and both a front and side porch.

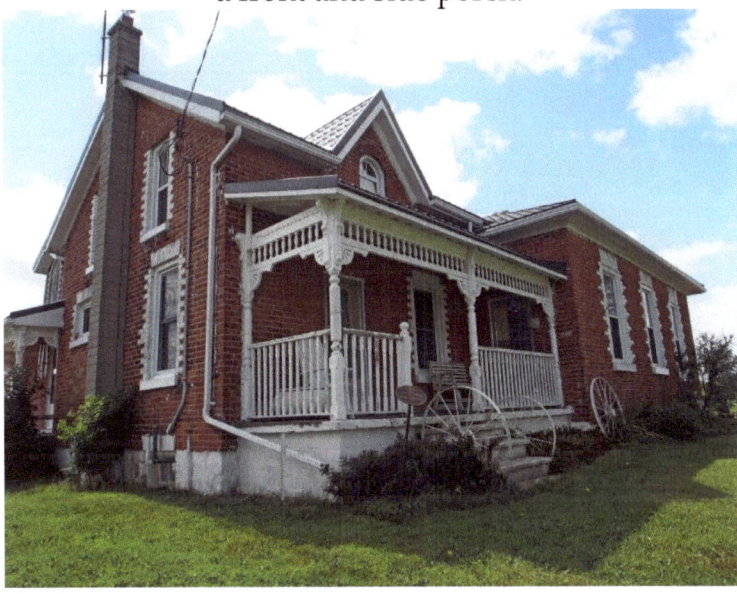

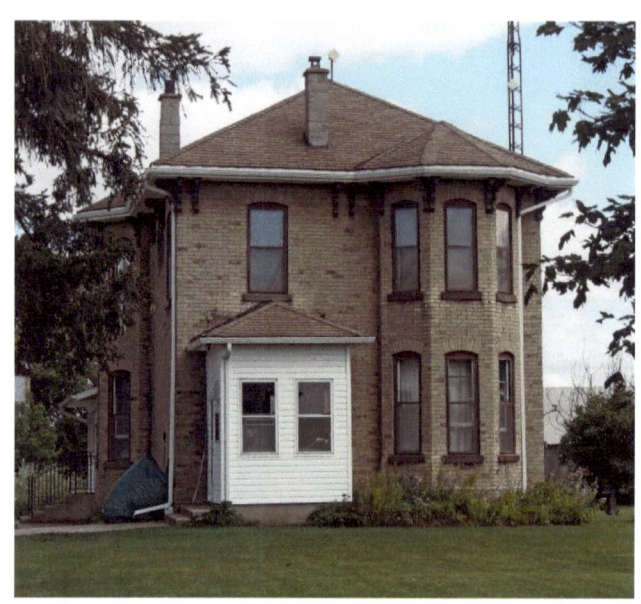

398 West Quarter Townline Road – two-storey bay window, paired cornice brackets

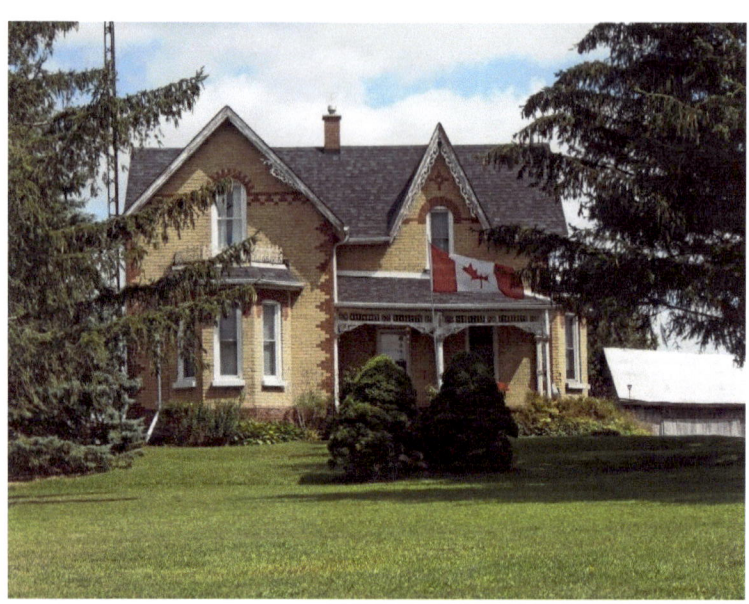

378 West Quarter Townline Road – Gothic Revival, dichromatic brickwork

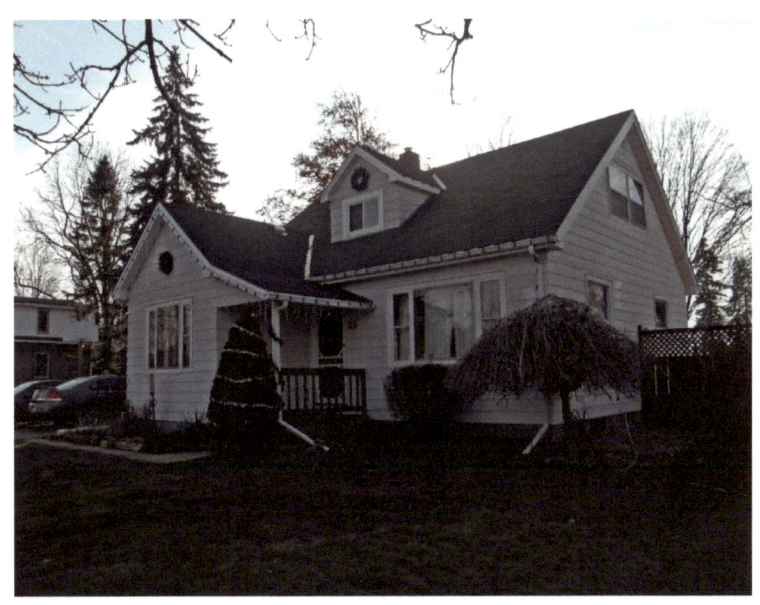

23 Minshall Drive – verge board trim on gable, dormer in attic

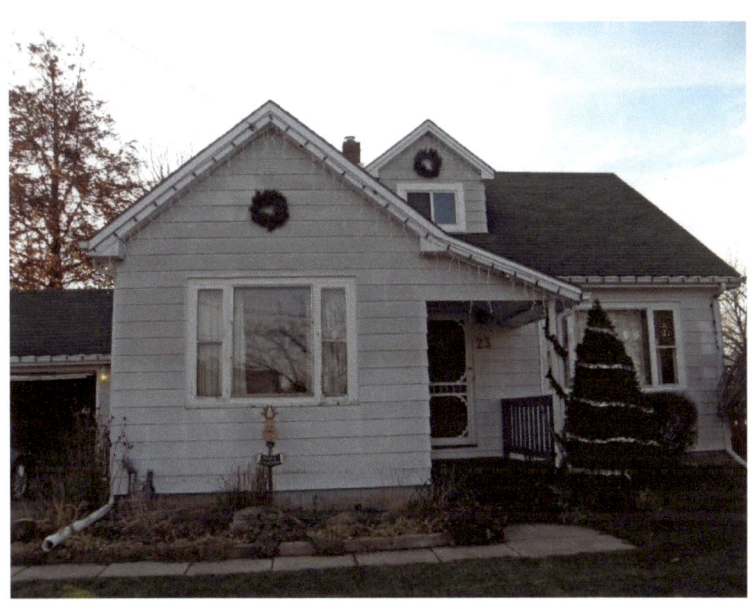

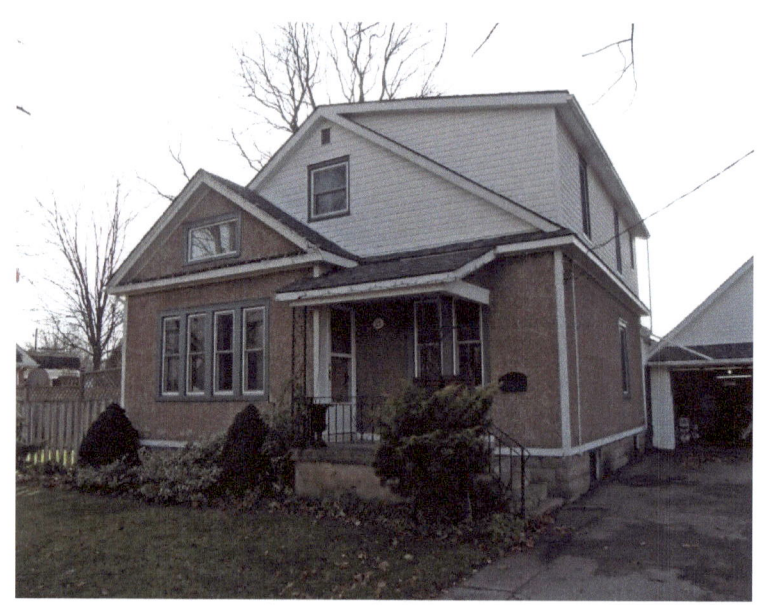

21 Minshall Drive

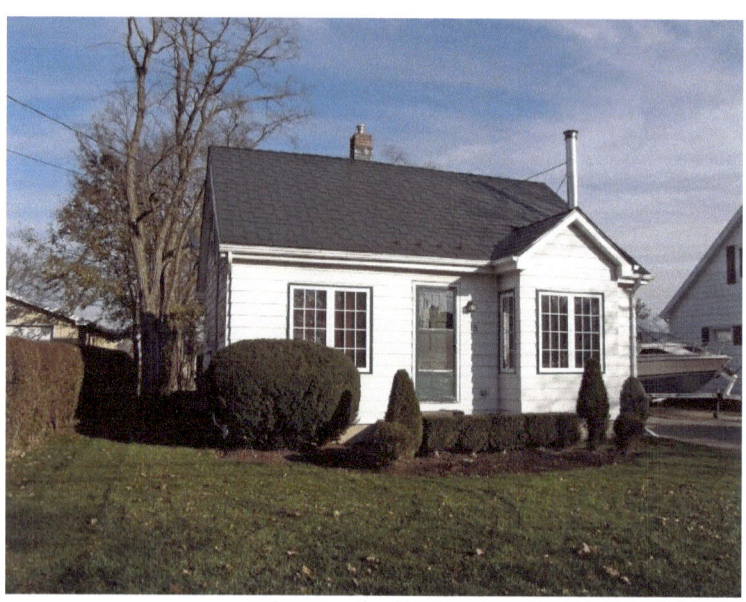

18 Minshall Drive

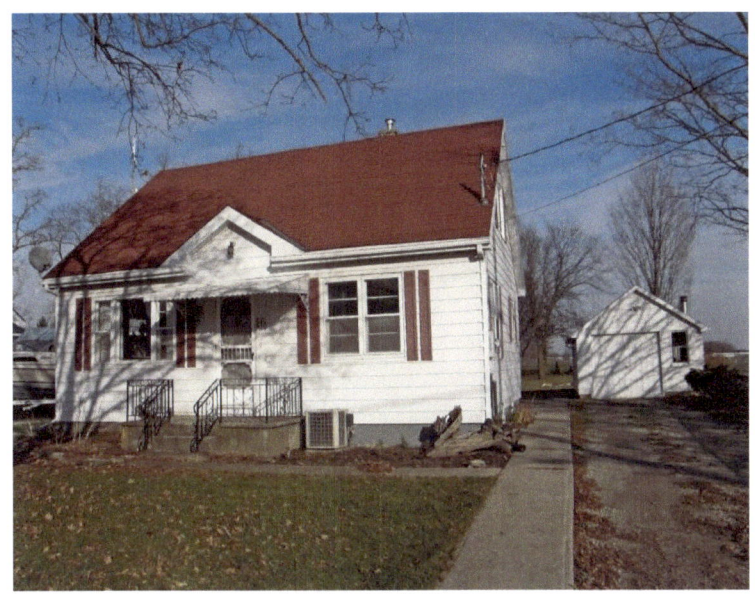

16 Minshall Drive

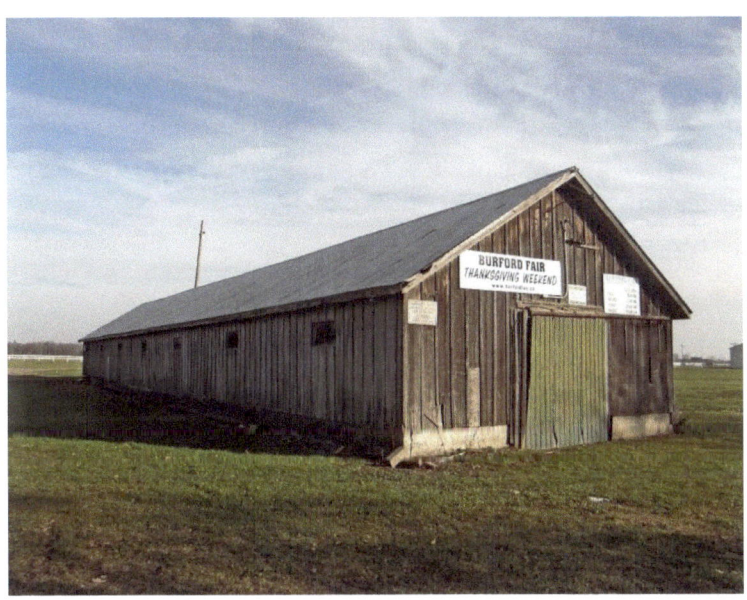

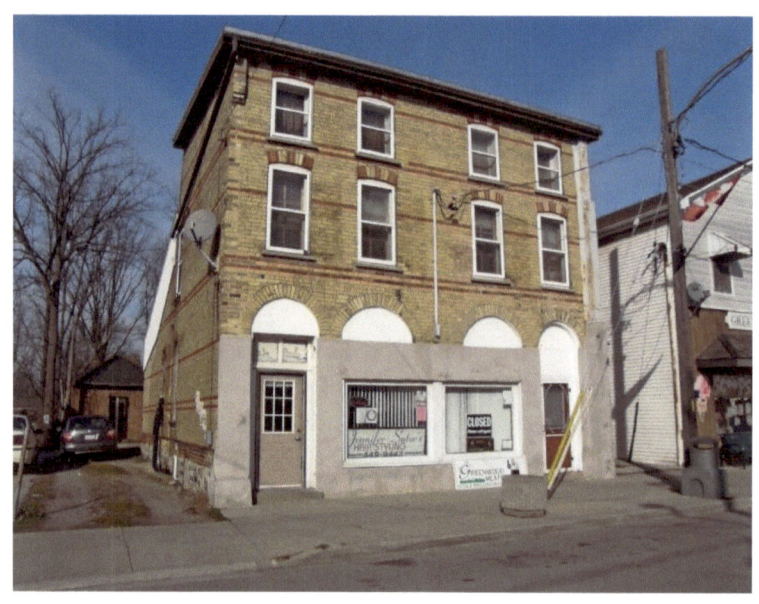

124 King Street – string courses, dichromatic brickwork

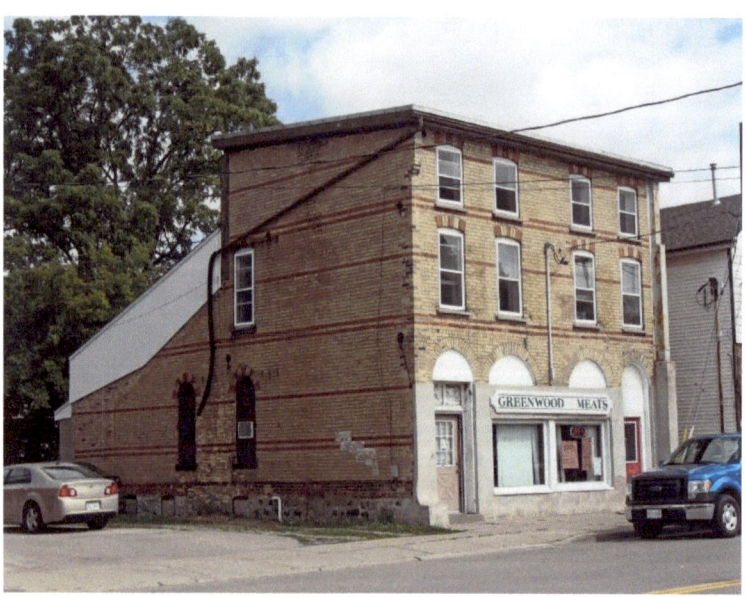

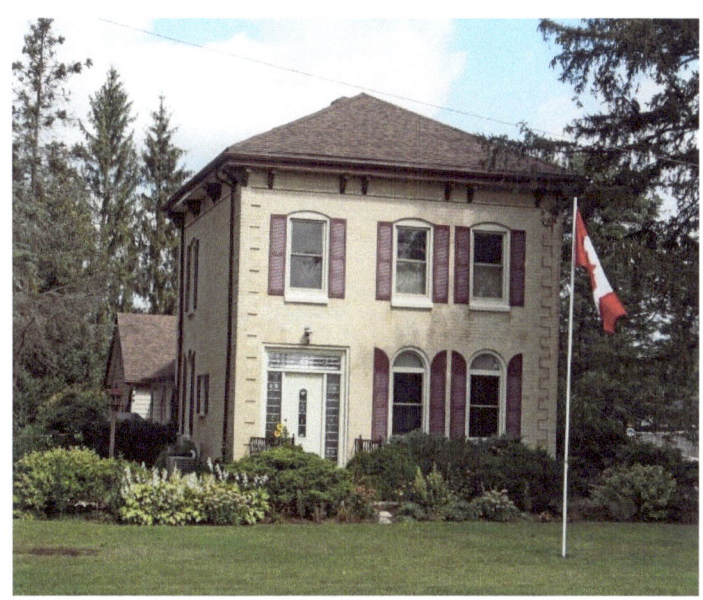

49 King Street – hipped roof, cornice brackets, corner quoins, sidelights and transom window

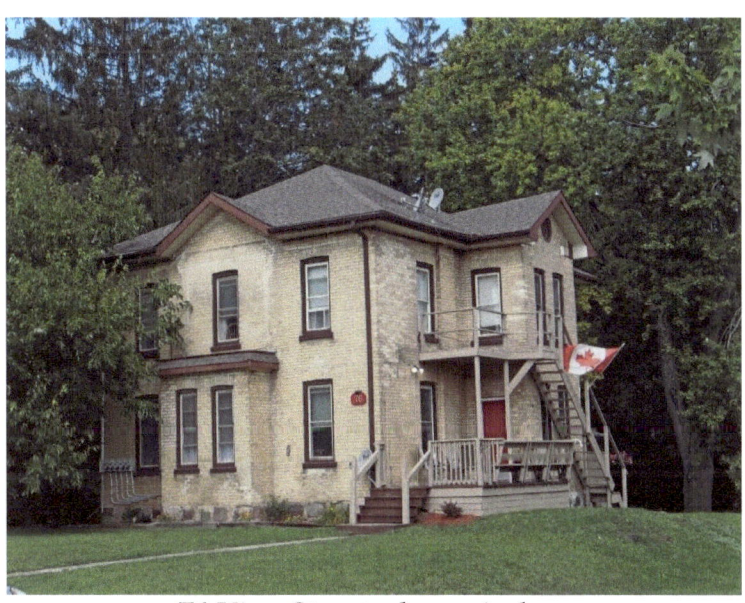

76 King Street – bay window

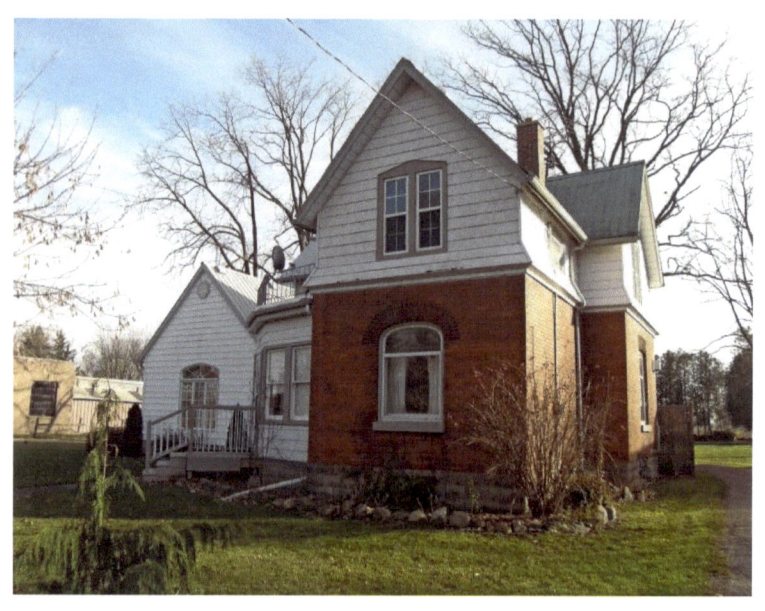

79 King Street

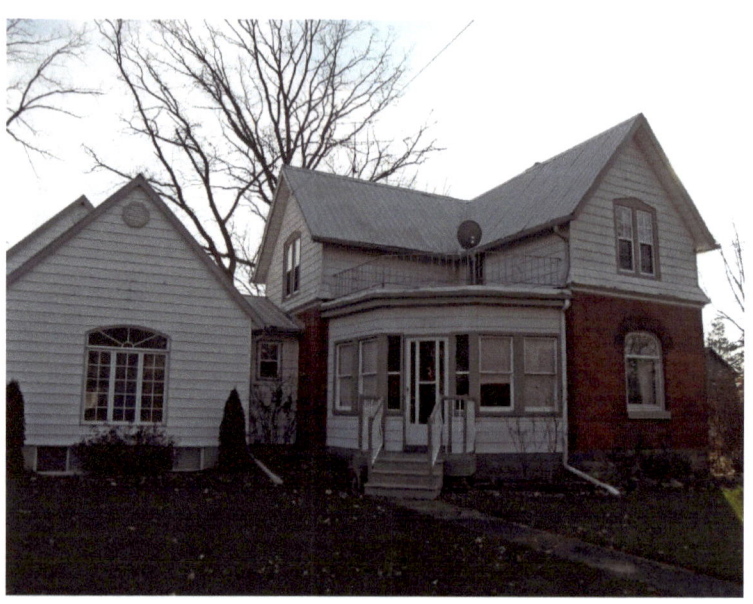

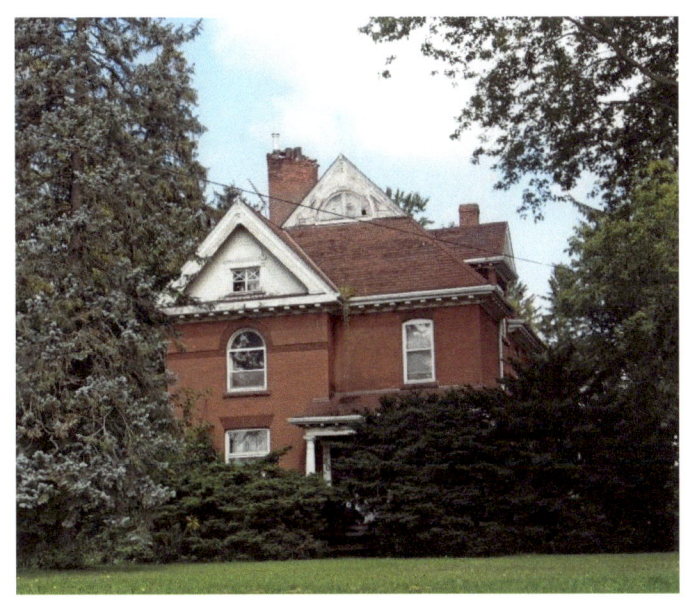

80 King Street – Queen Anne style

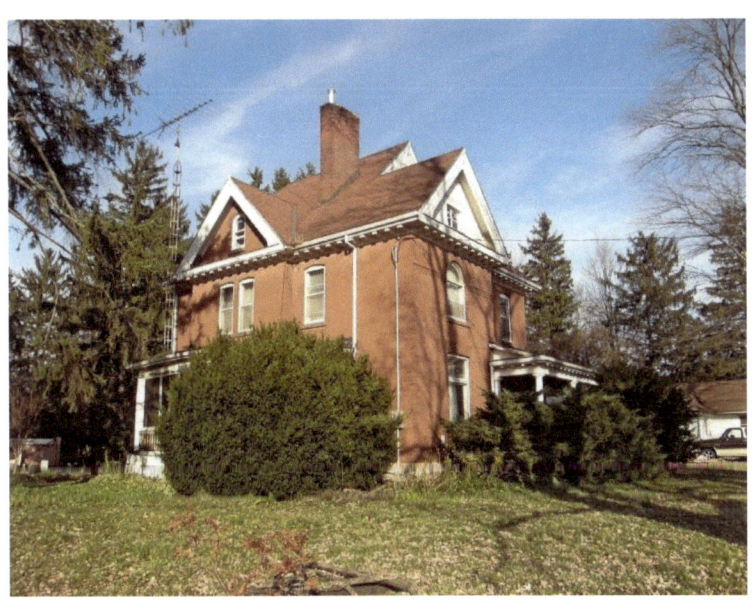

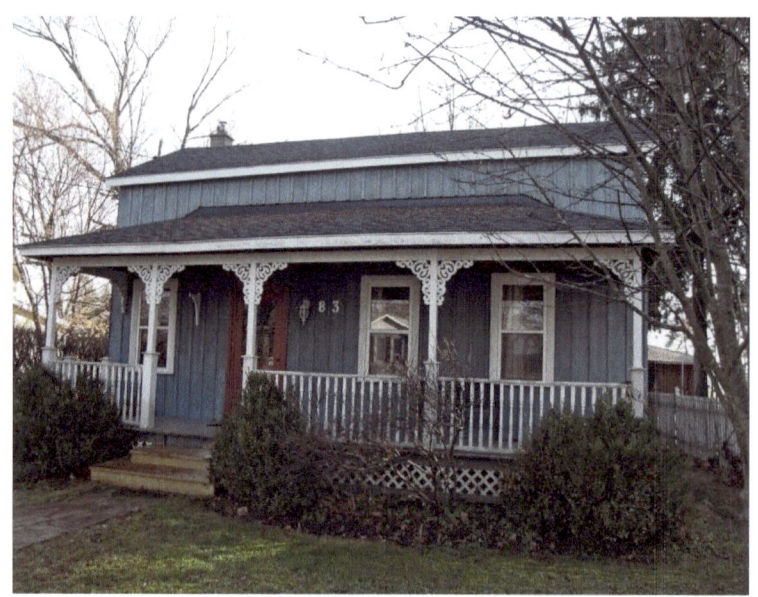

83 King Street

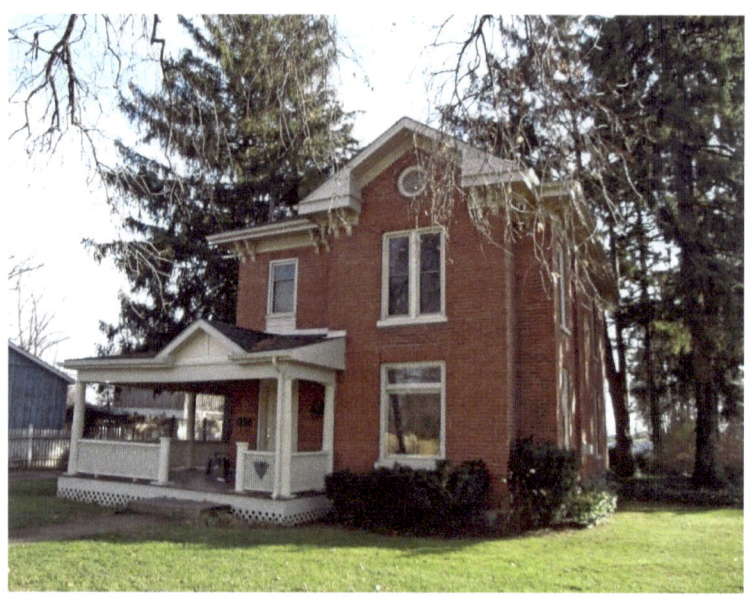

85 King Street

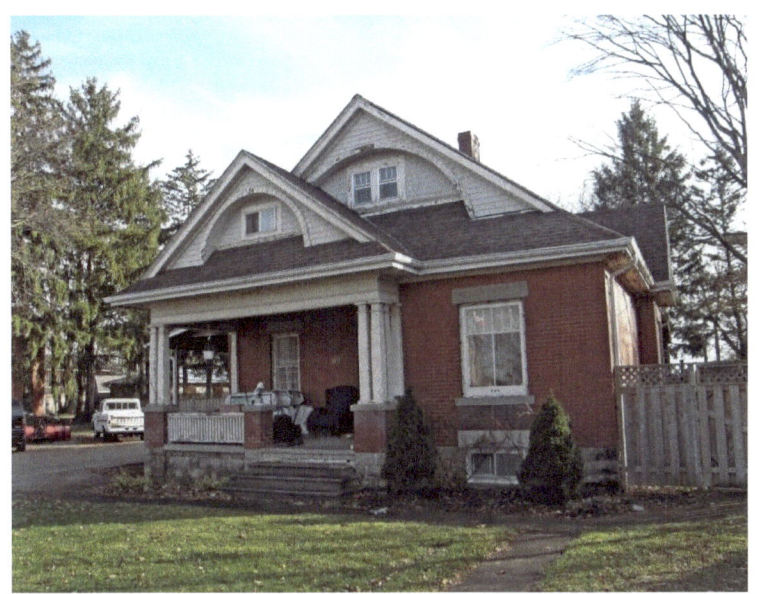

89 King Street - vernacular

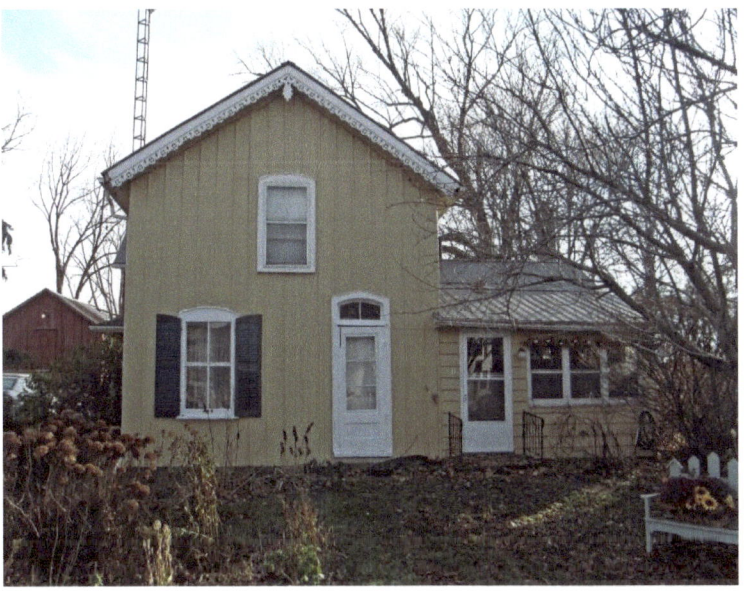

King Street – Gothic, verge board trim, transom window

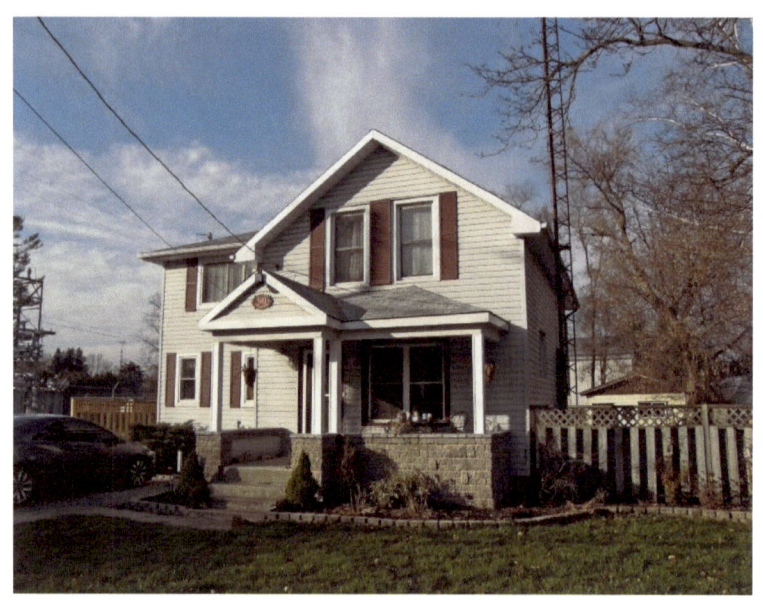

90 King Street - pediment

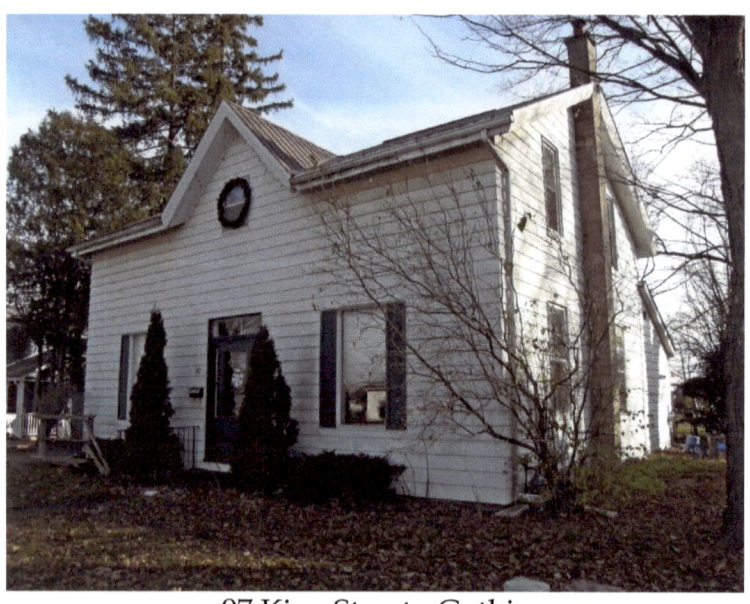

97 King Street - Gothic

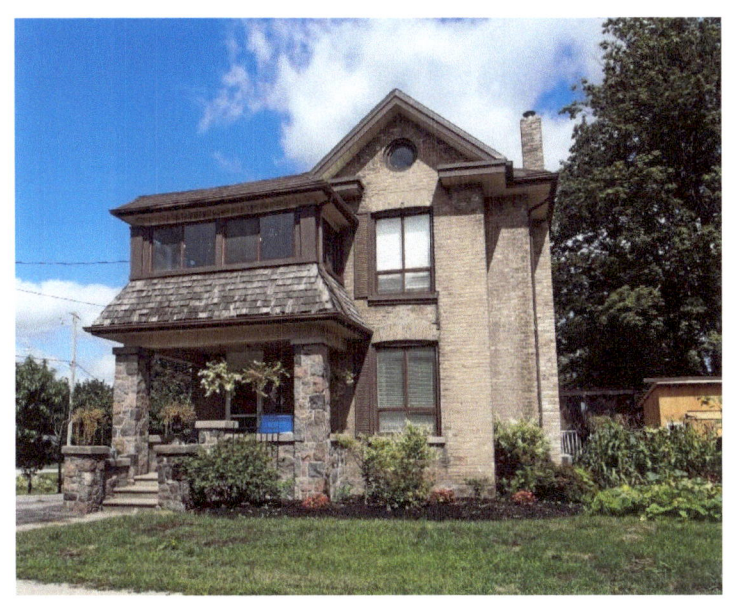

96 King Street

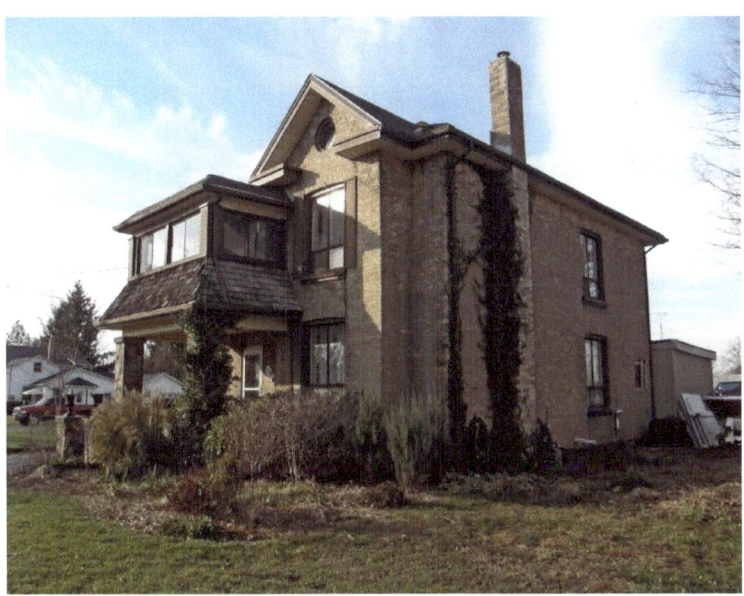

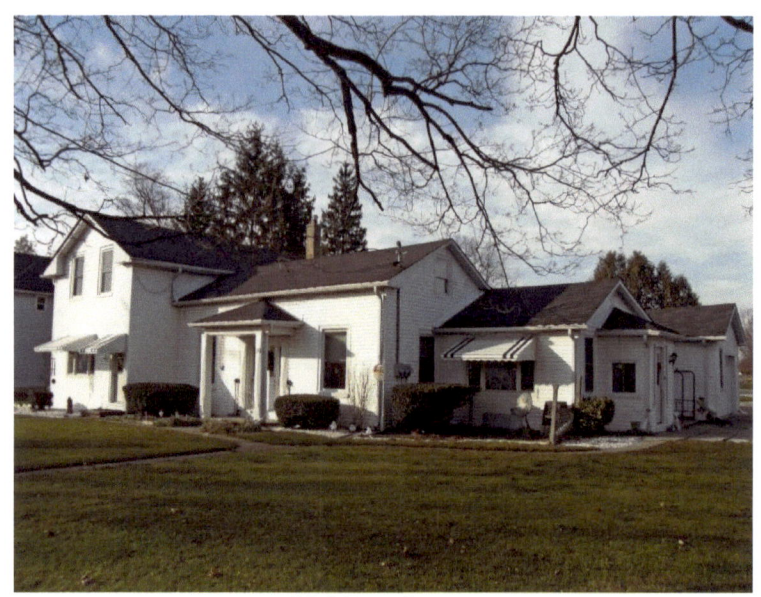

98 King Street

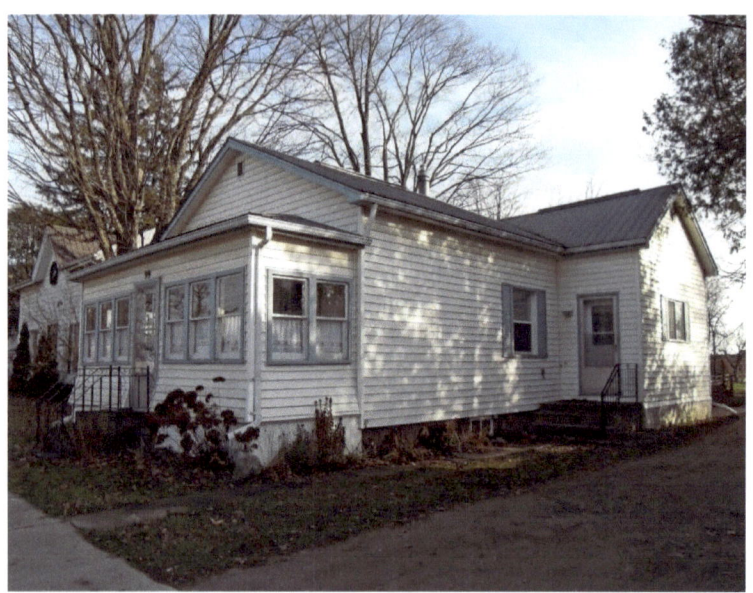

99 King Street

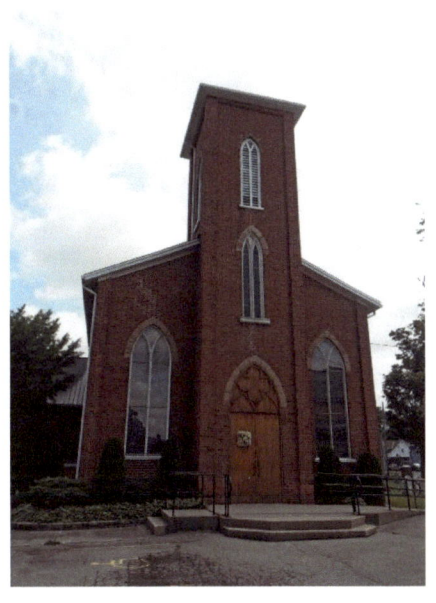

104 King Street – Holy Trinity Anglican Church – A.D. 1851 – Gothic, lancet windows

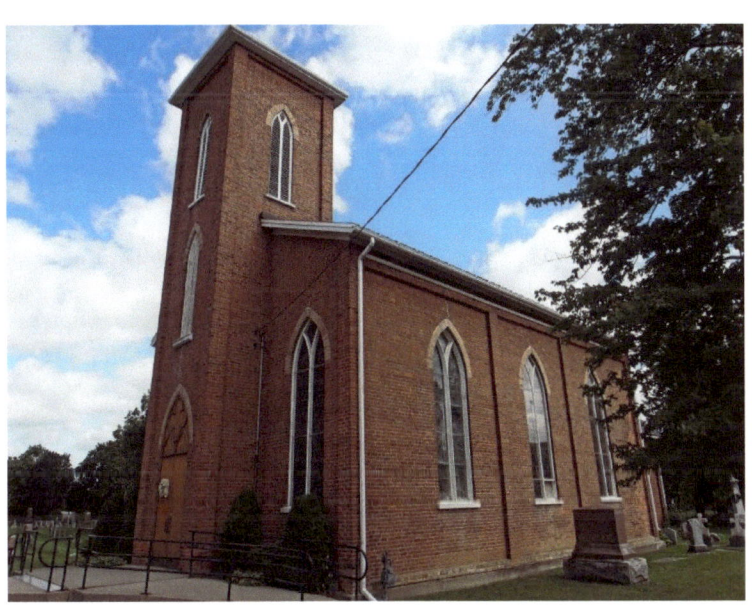

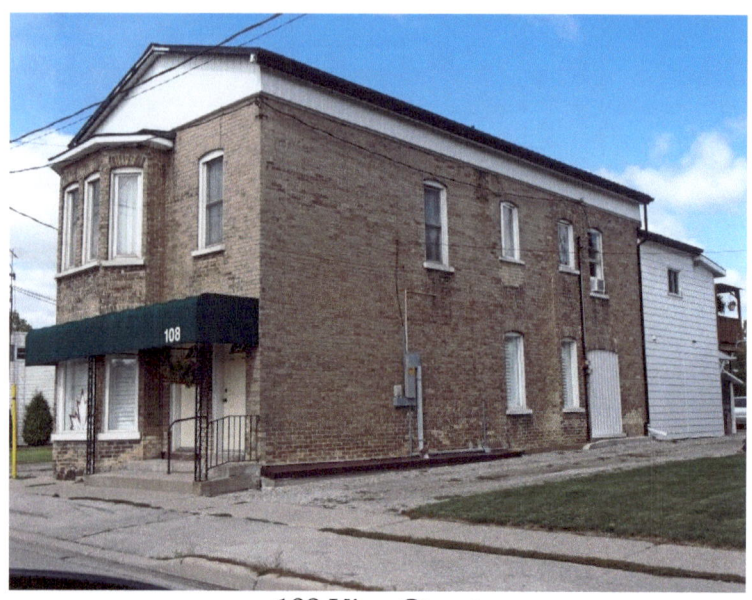

108 King Street

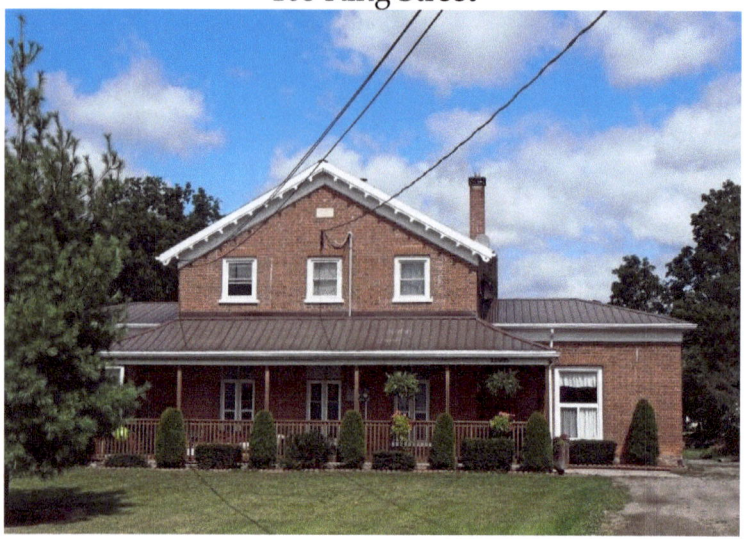

110 King Street – Dr. Hervey Ross House – 1851 – It is usually called "The Miller House" and is a rare example of a Regency winged temple building. It is called a "winged plan" because it has a one and a half storey central body with flanking one-storey wings. Decorative features are fancy verge board along the front gable and French casement style windows.

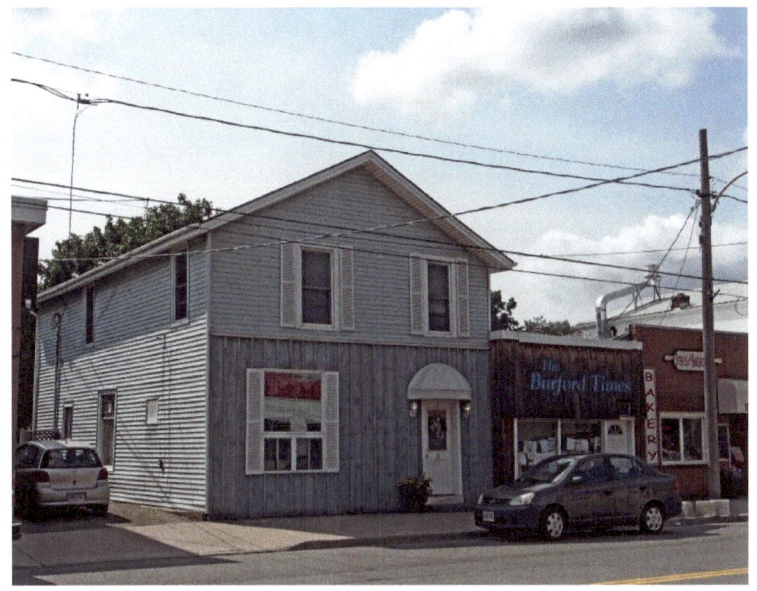

115 King Street

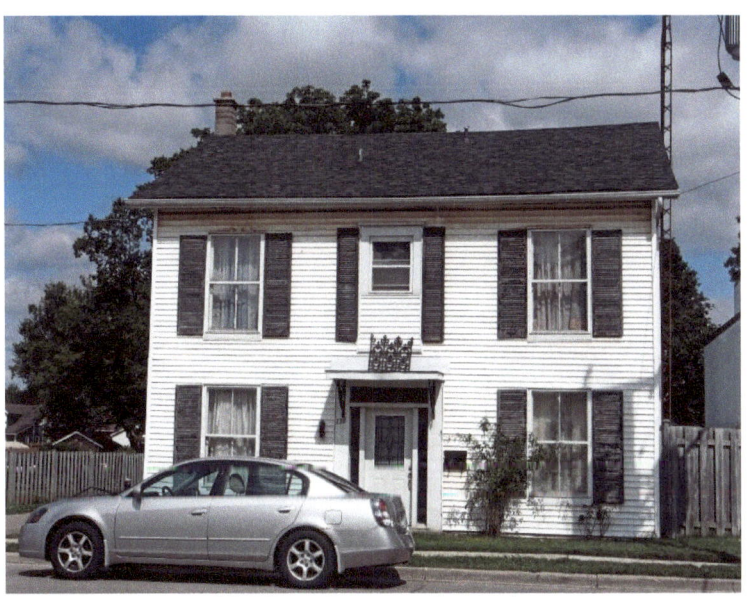

130 King Street - Georgian

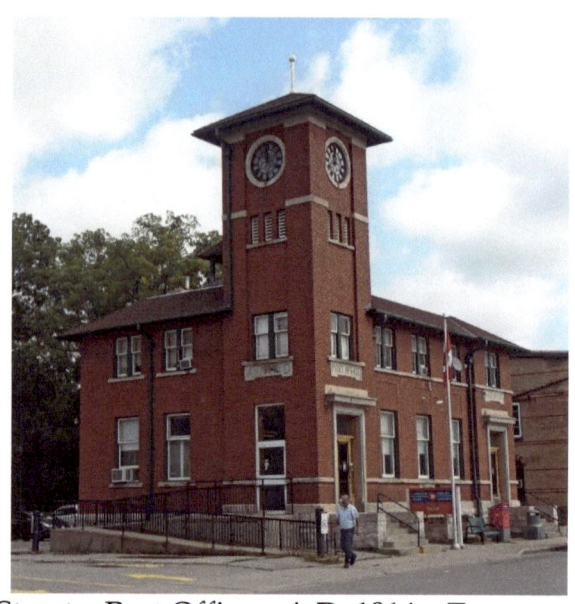

126 King Street – Post Office – A.D. 1914 – Two-storey smooth red brick structure has ashlar stone lintels and stringcourses at the window lines. It is sometimes called Edwardian in style because it was built during the reign of King Edward VII. The clock tower is a landmark for the business district.

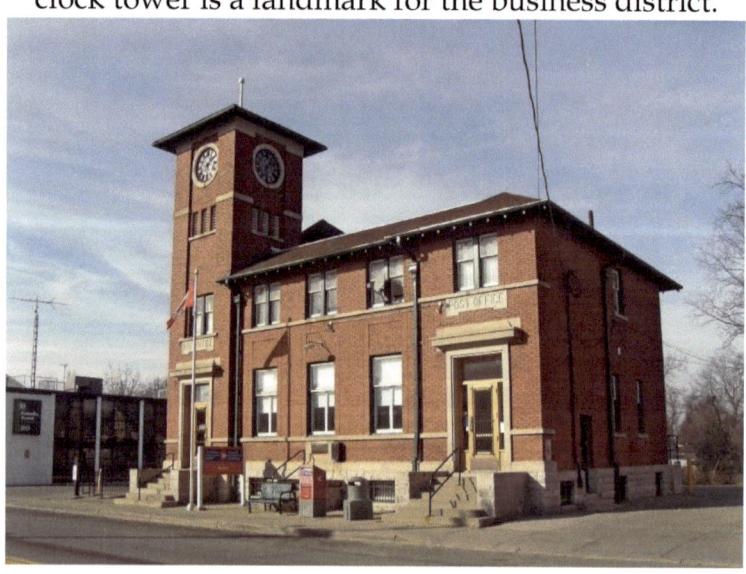

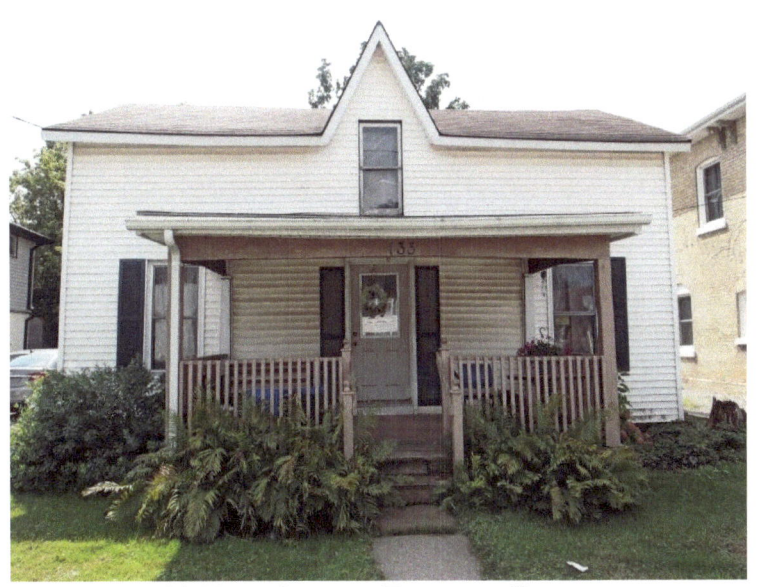

133 King Street – Regency Cottage

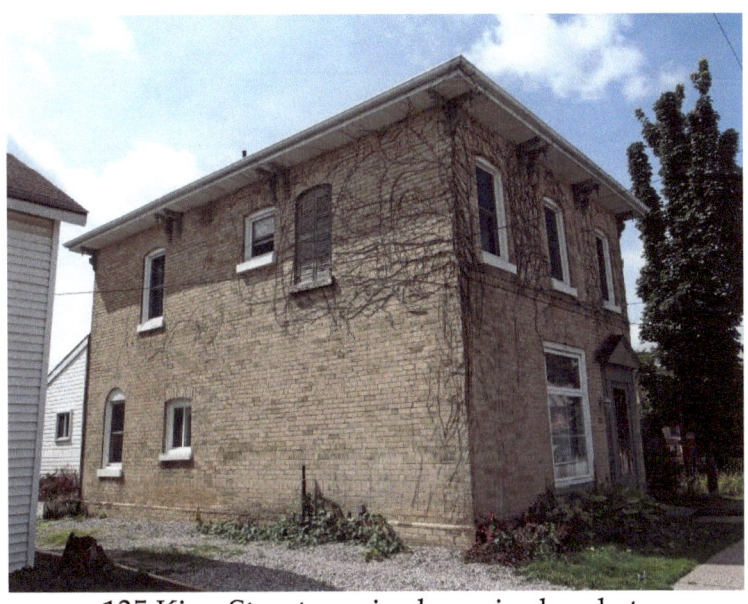

135 King Street – paired cornice brackets

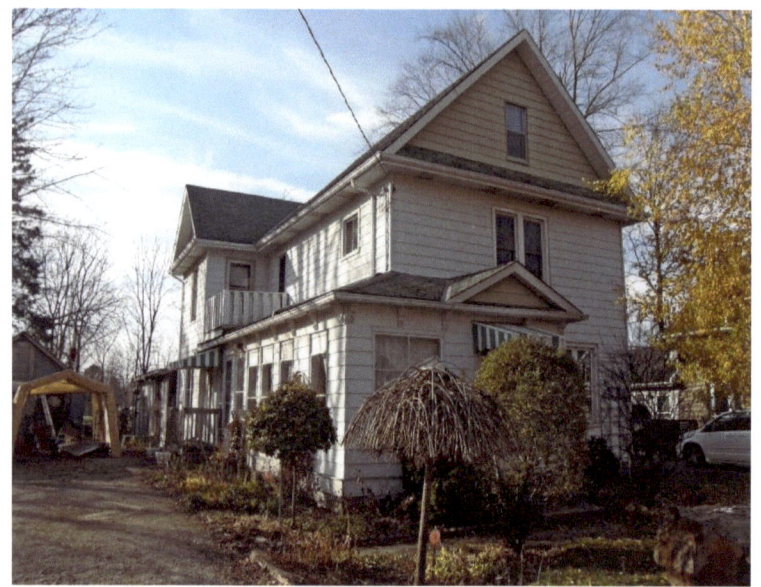

King Street - pediment

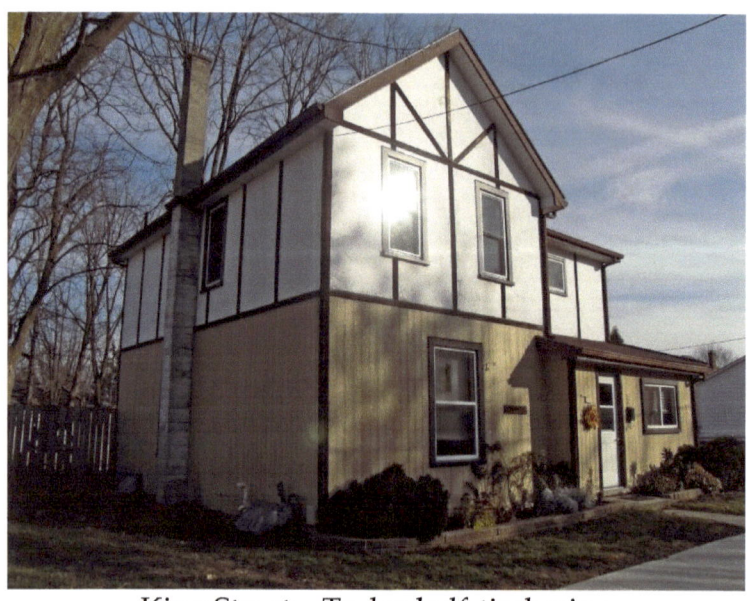

King Street – Tudor half-timbering

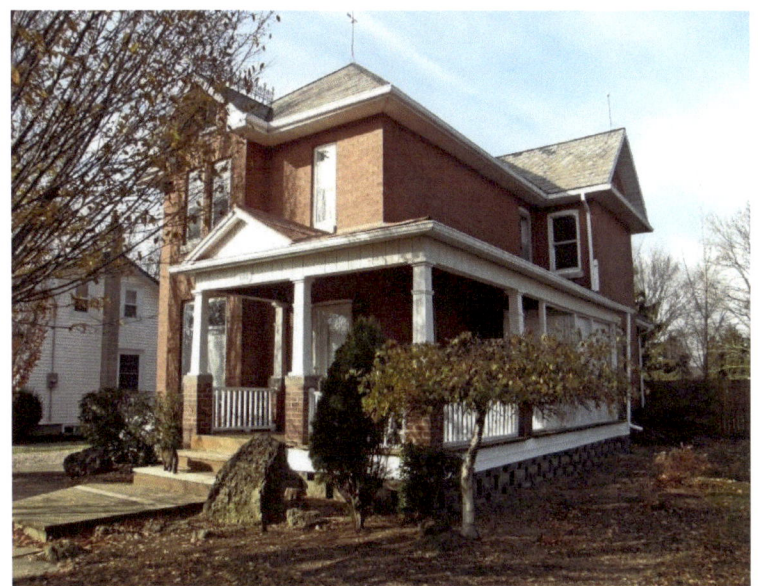

138 King Street - pediment

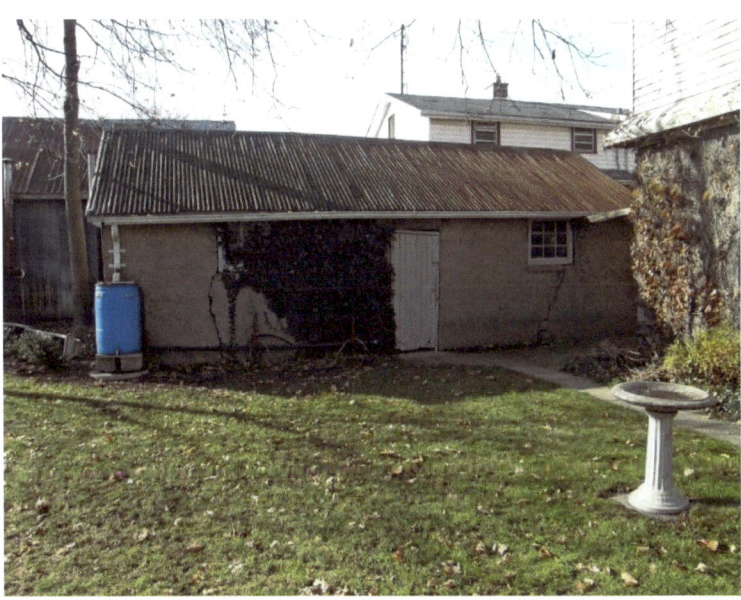

Old stone building on Alexander Street behind 139 King Street

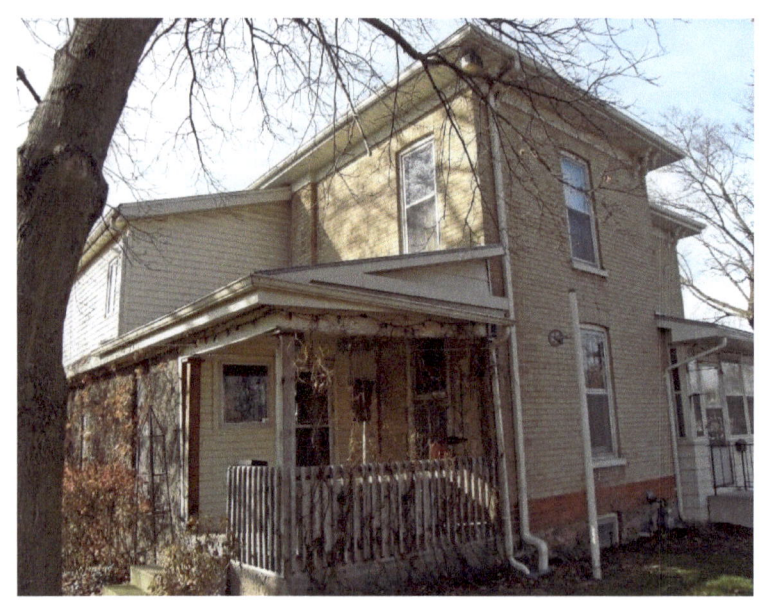

139 King Street

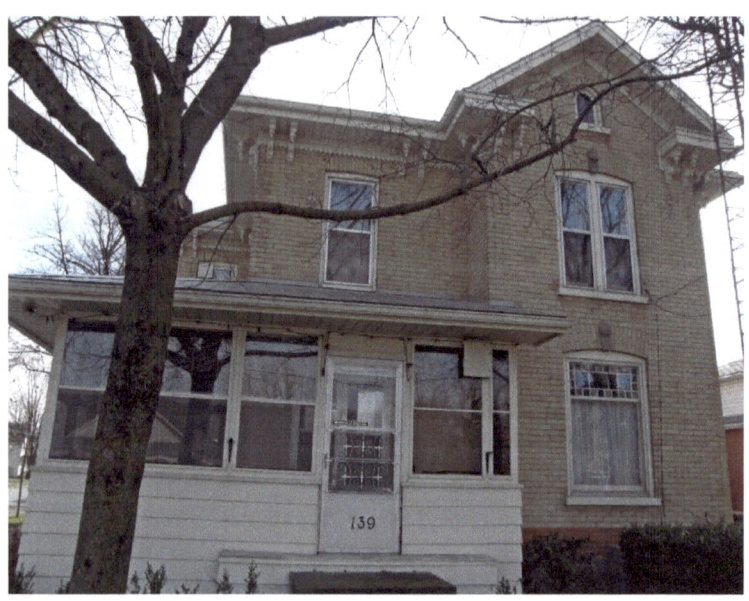

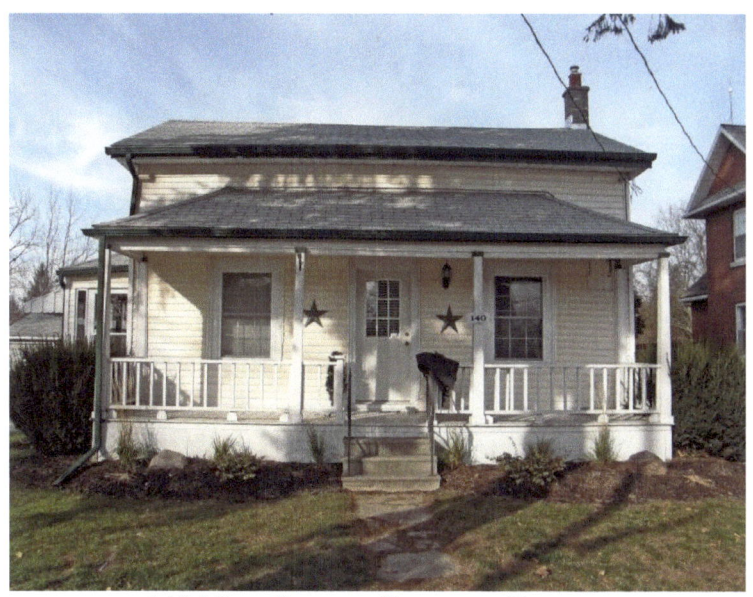

140 King Street – Regency Cottage

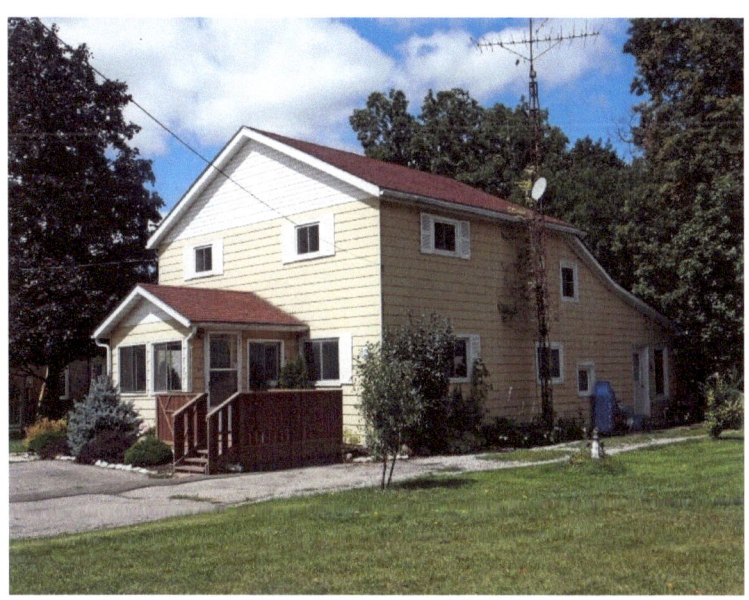

King Street - saltbox

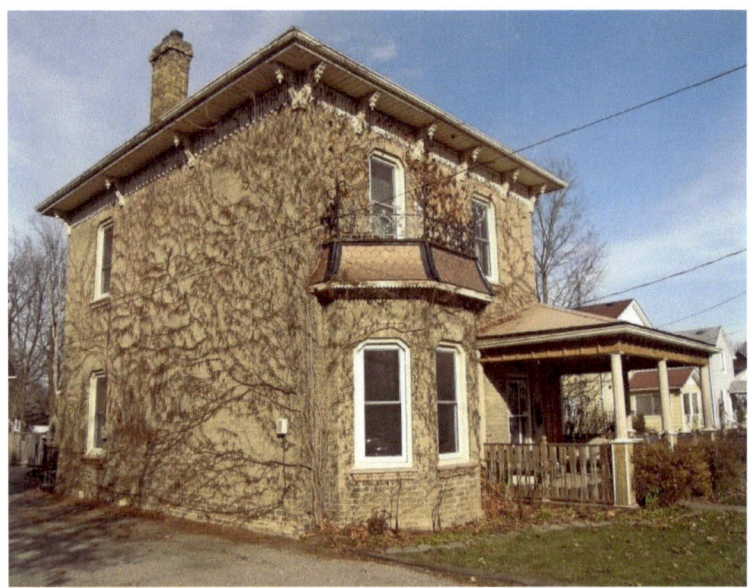
146 King Street – bay window, cornice brackets

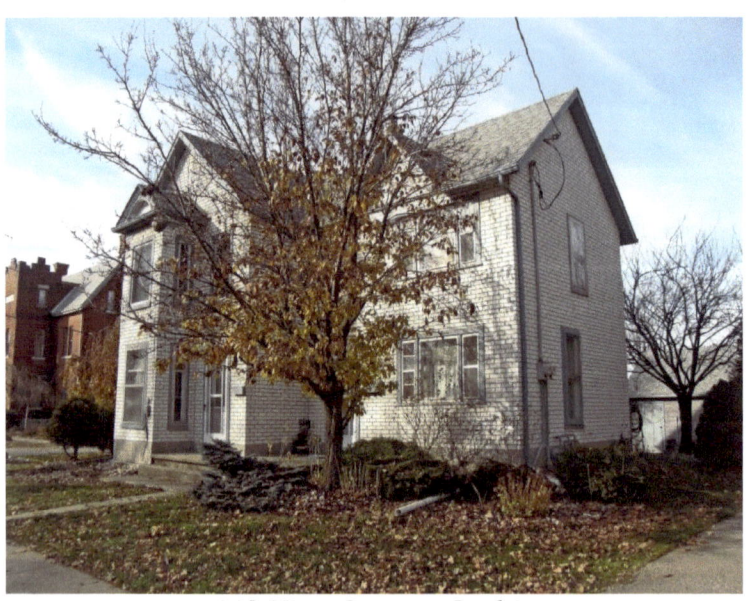
148 King Street - Gothic

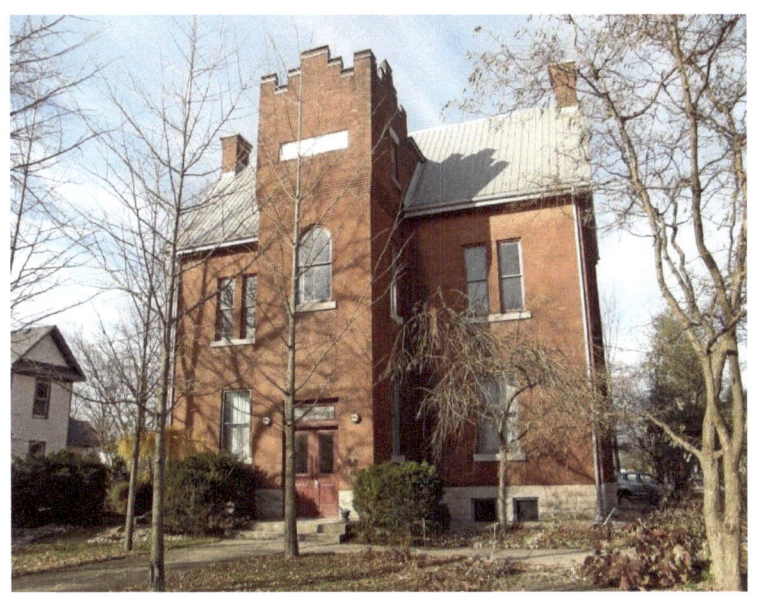

150 King Street – Armoury – 1906 – The central tower has a Roman arched window and Gothic detail as well as battlementing. The double front doors have a stained glass transom. It was used by the 1st Cavalry 2nd 10th Brant Dragoons for training and recreation. It served as a hospital during the flu epidemic of 1918 and a temporary high school in 1921. During the War of 1812, Burford became an important post, being located between Ancaster and Detroit. The military parade ground was located on this property and occupied most of what is now the residential block between William and Jarvis Streets.

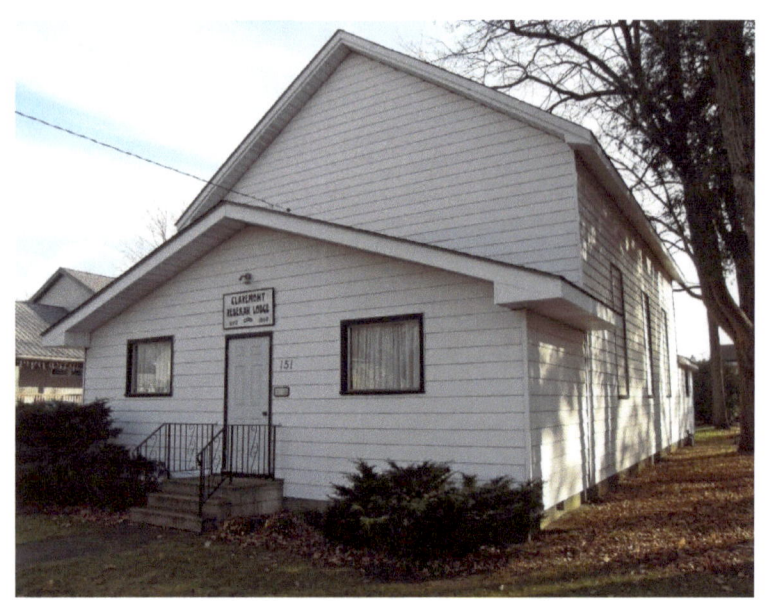

151 King Street - Vernacular

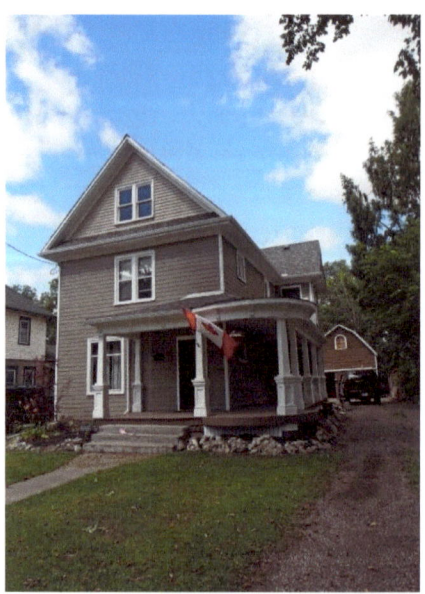

152 King Street – Edwardian

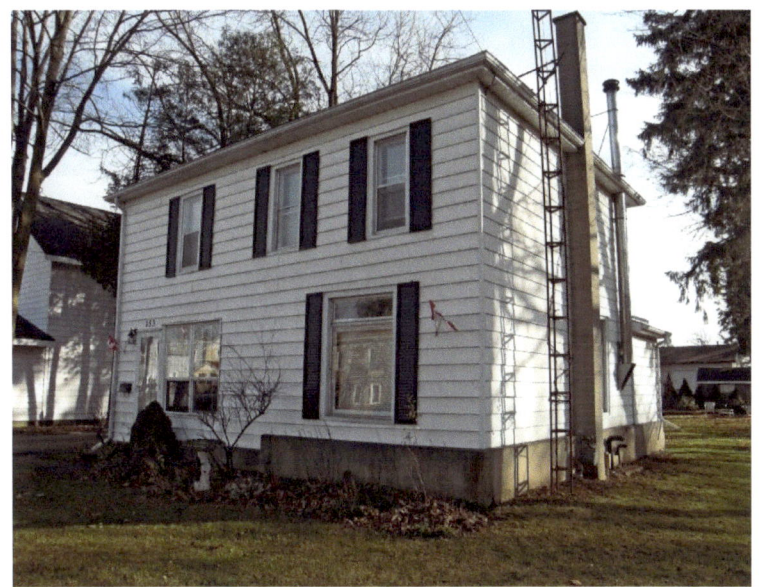

153 King Street

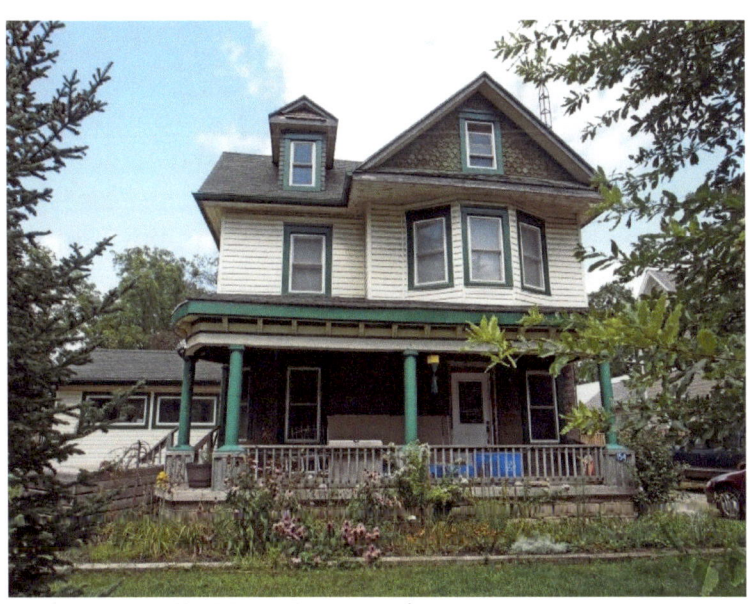

154 King Street – dormer in attic

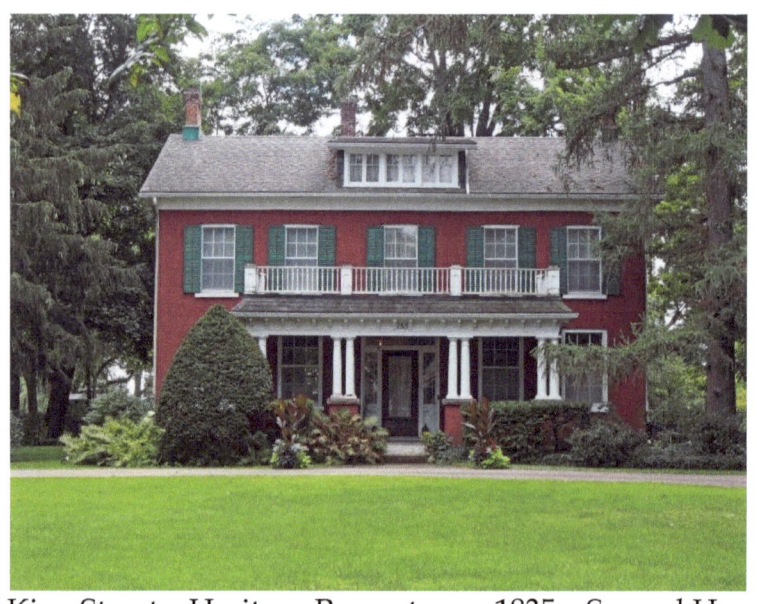

155 King Street – Heritage Property – c. 1835 – Sprowl House – Doric columns support a sleeper veranda used on hot summer nights. The six over six windows are original. This is the former home of A.D. Muir who was active in the militia and joined the Burford Troop of Cavalry in 1881. In 1813, following the defeat of the Canadians at the battle of Moraviantown (west of London), General Proctor persuaded a group of nearly 3000 native warriors and their families to retreat with him to a powerful fort which he claimed to be at Burford. Some of this group encamped here (across from the military parade grounds) while the rest of the group was located west of the village by the creek.

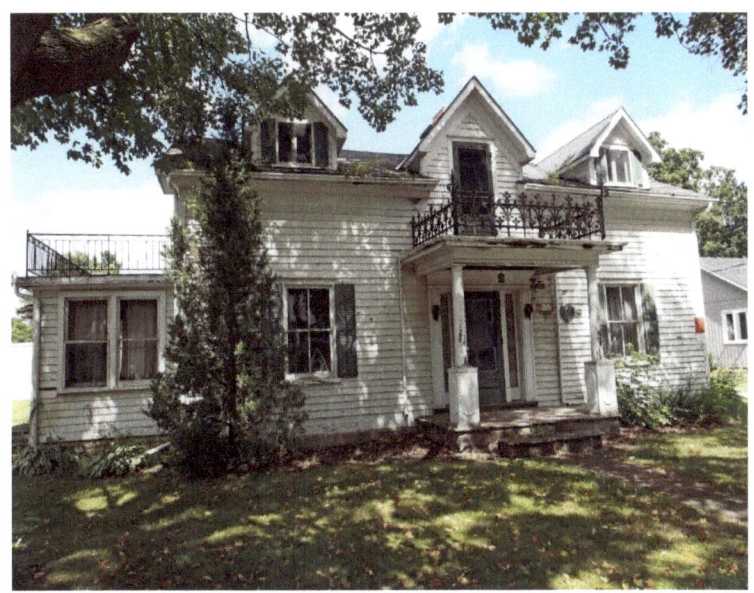

158 King Street – dormers, iron cresting around second floor balcony

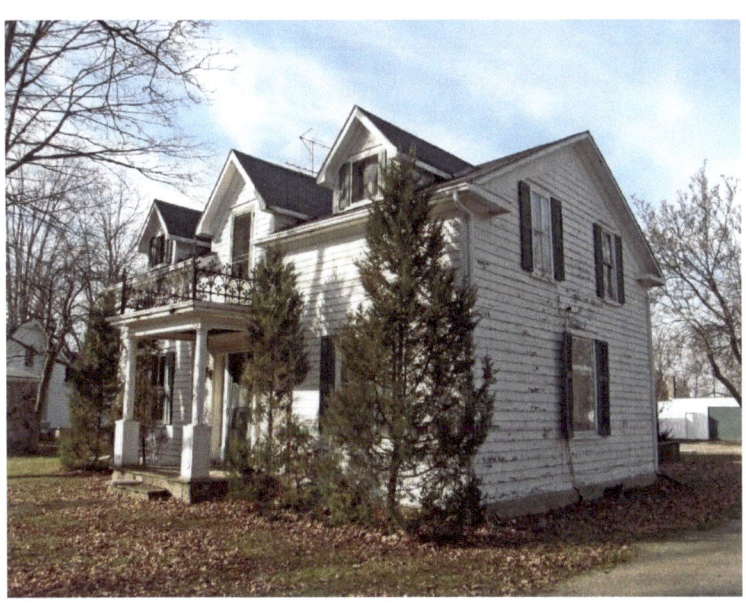

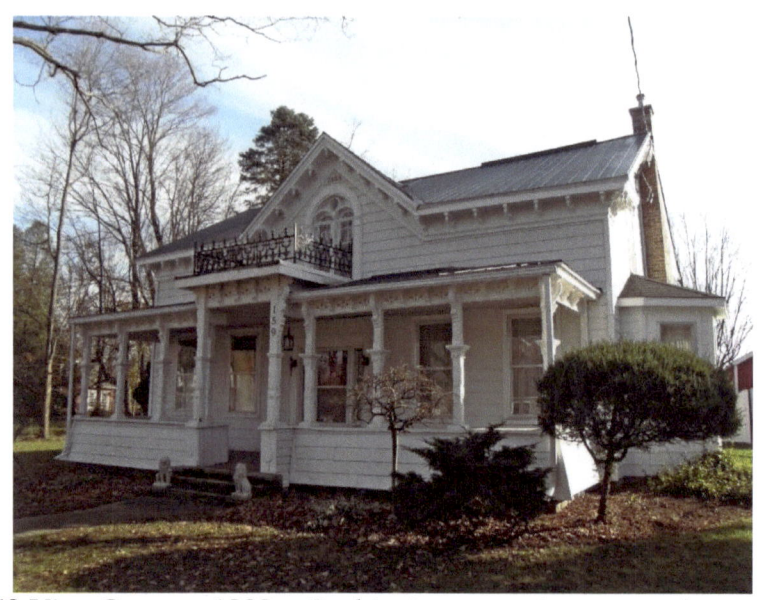

159 King Street – 1888 – Gothic, iron cresting around second floor balcony, cornice brackets, stenciling and decorative veranda pillars, bay window on end of house

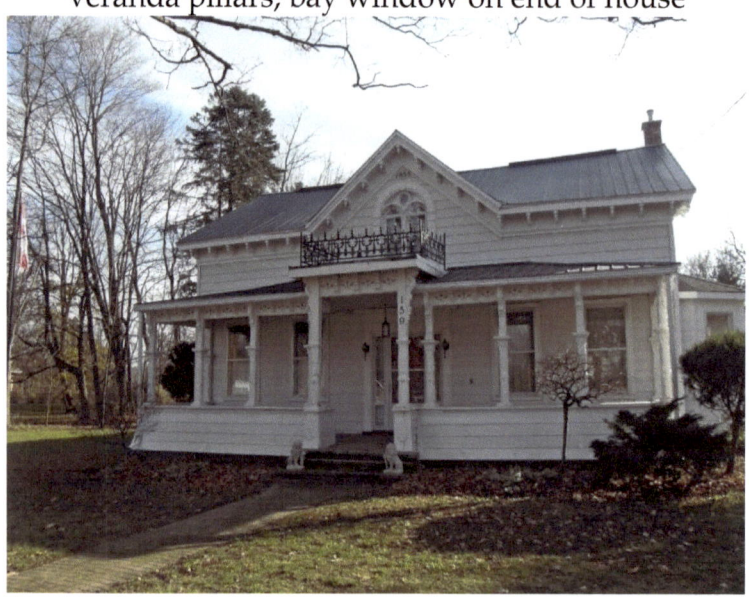

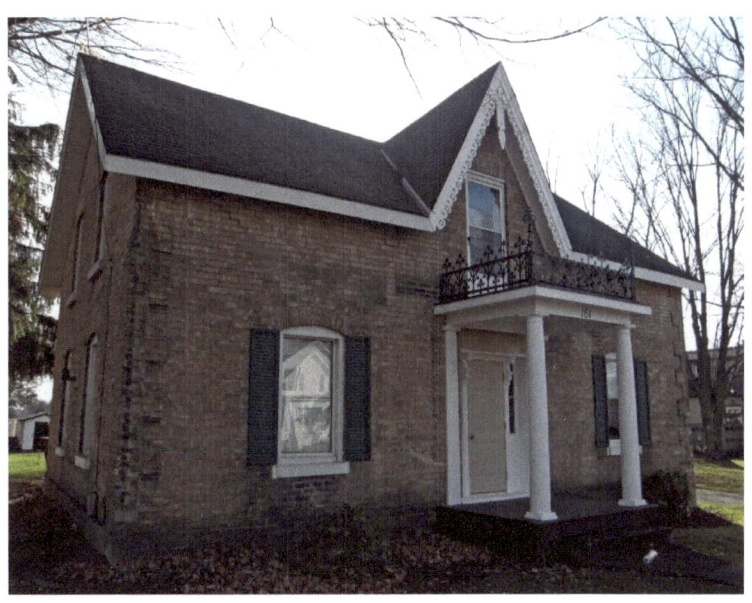

161 King Street – Gothic, iron cresting around second floor balcony, verge board trim and finial on gable, corner quoins

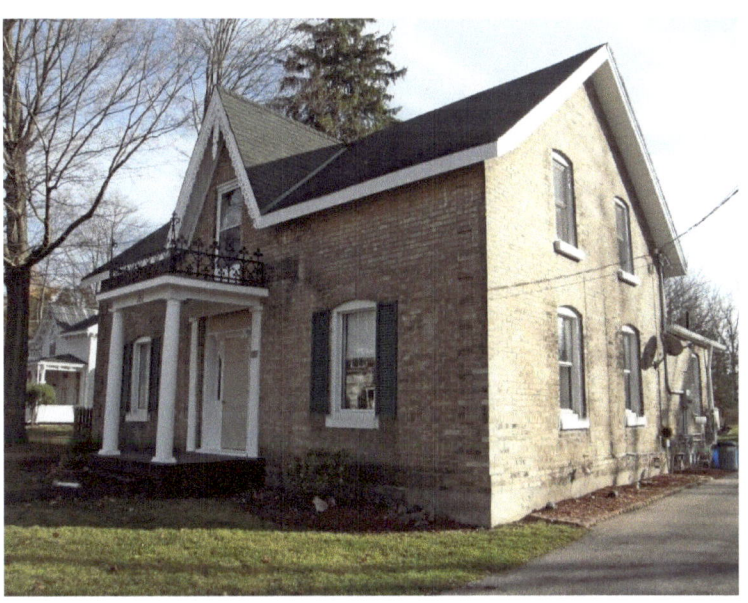

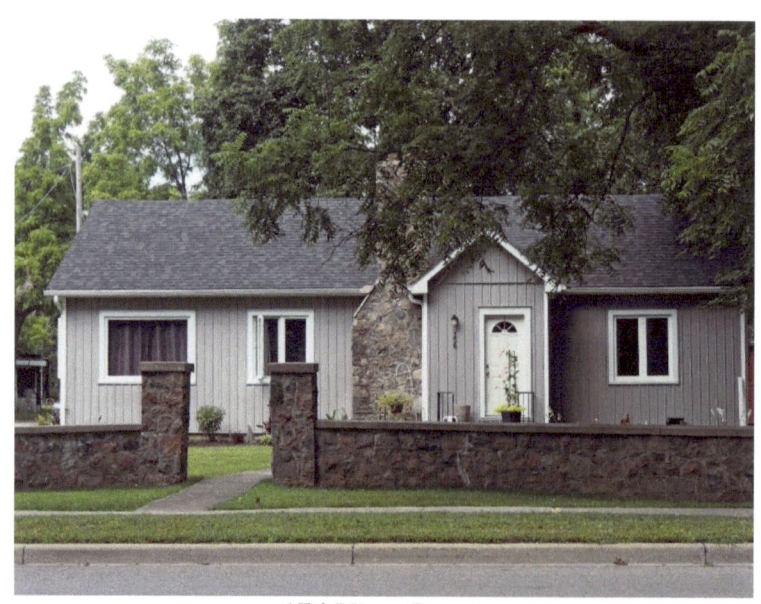

156 King Street

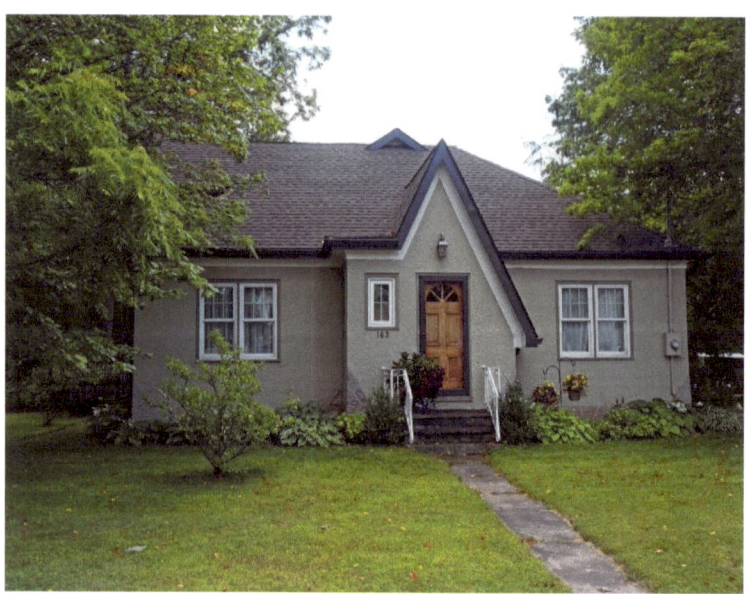

163 King Street

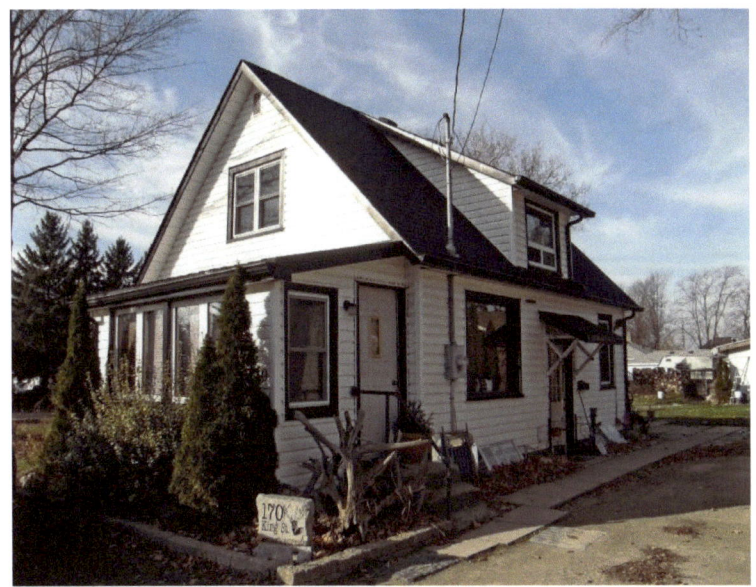

170 King Street

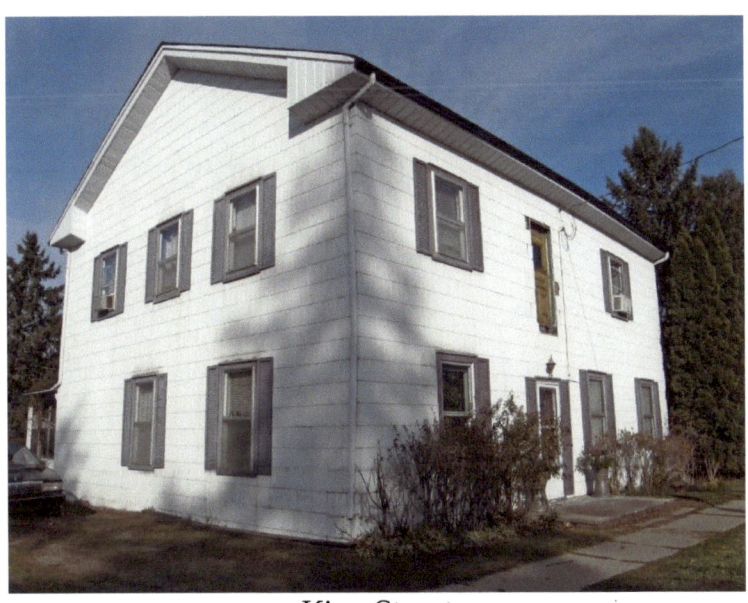

King Street

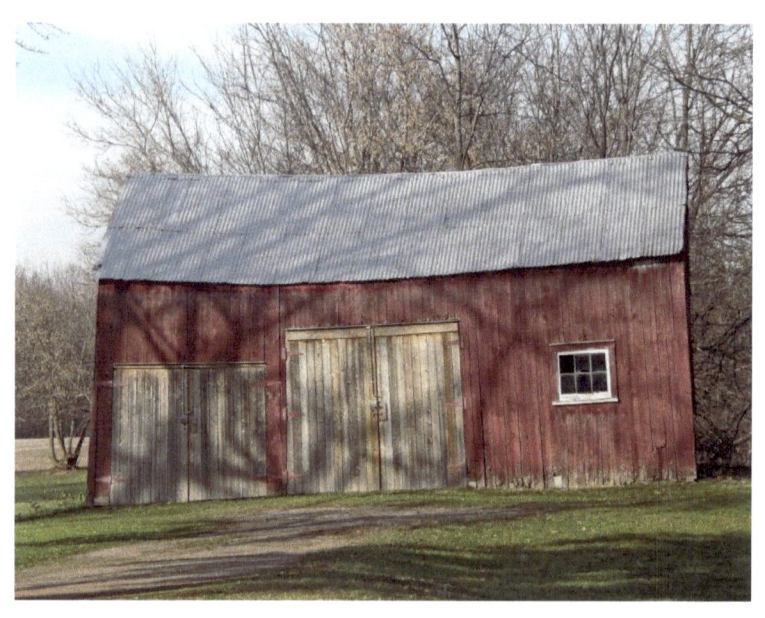

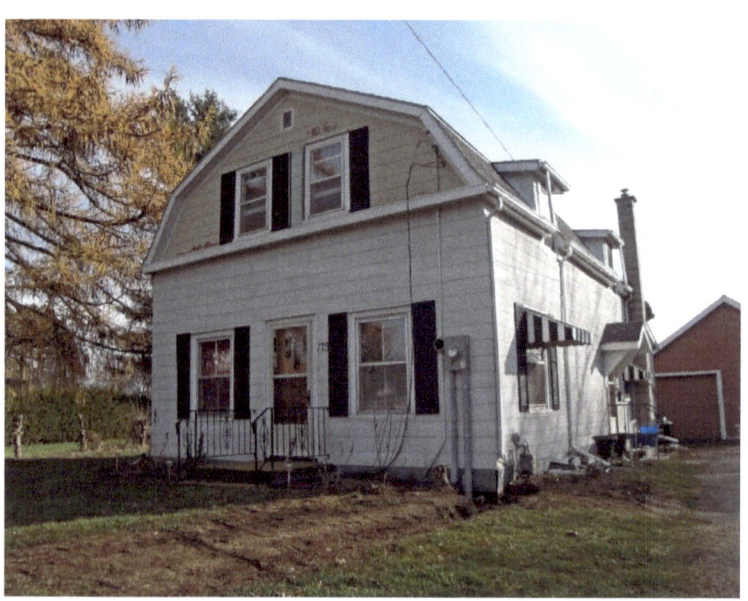

175 King Street – Neo-colonial – gambrel roof

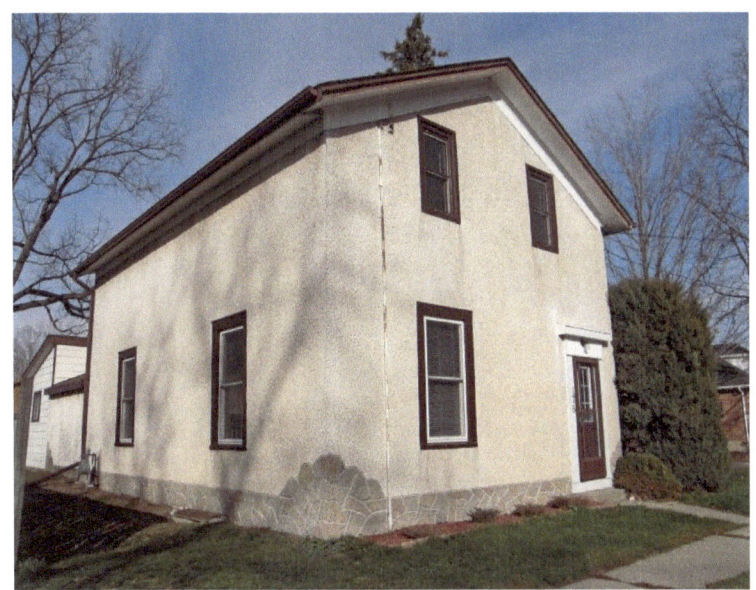

178 King Street

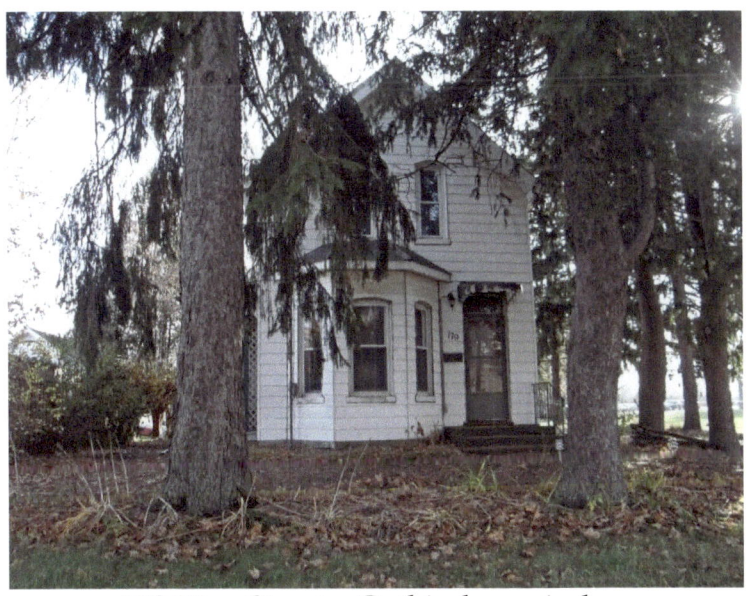

179 King Street – Gothic, bay window

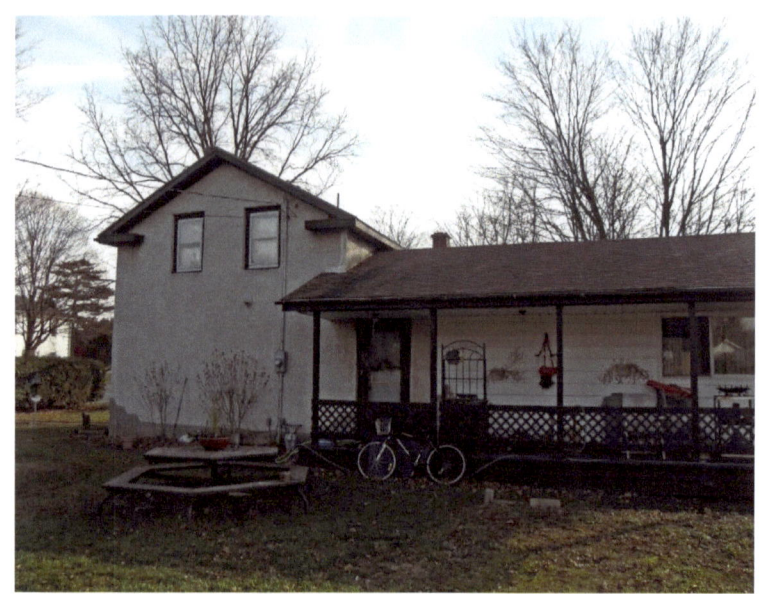

1 Maple Avenue North

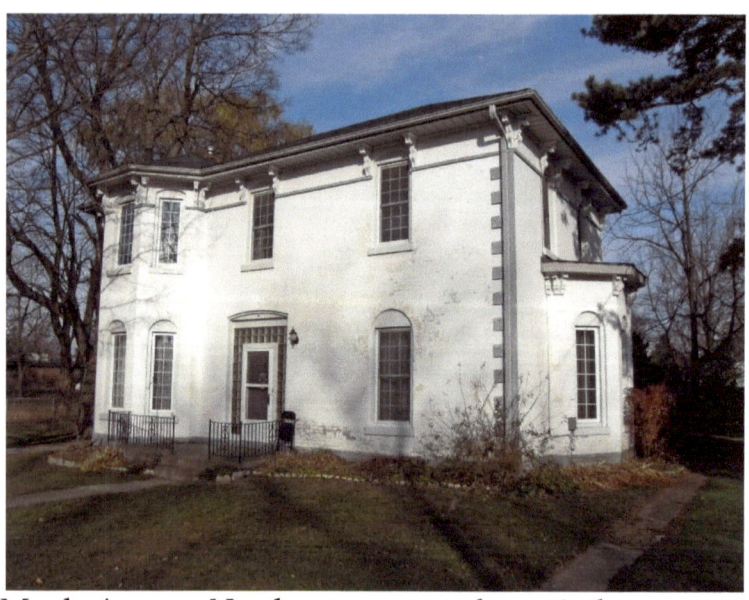

2 Maple Avenue North – two-storey bay windows, cornice brackets, corner quoins

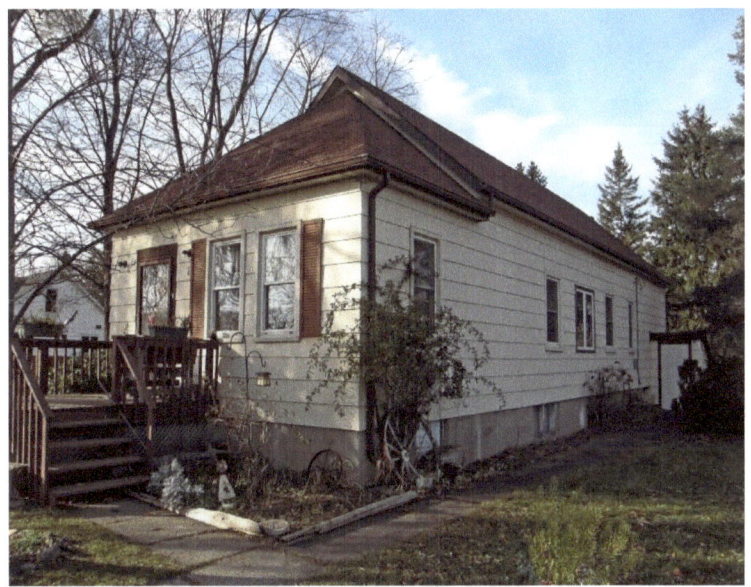

Maple Avenue North

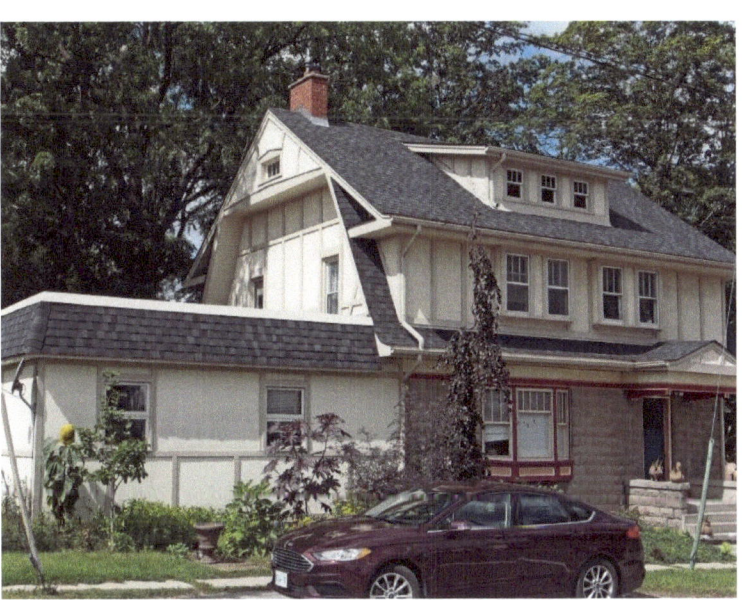

5 Maple Avenue North

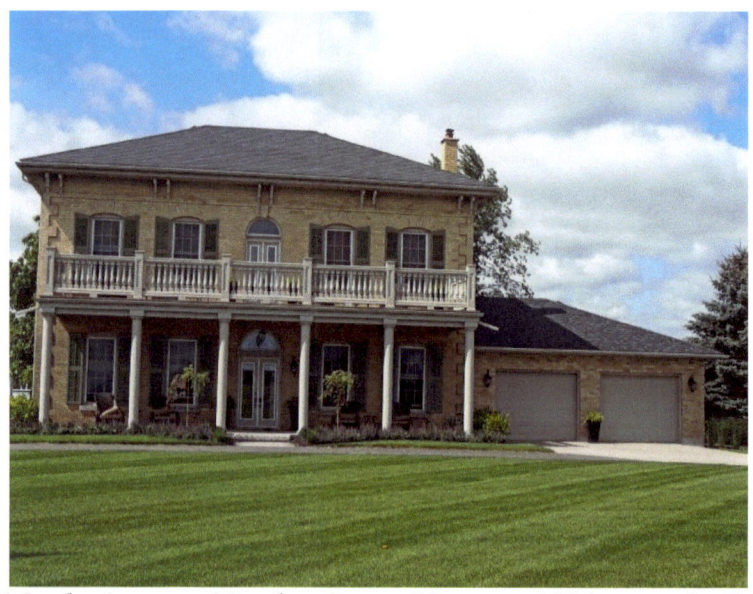

55 Maple Avenue North – Stuart House – 1886 – was built by Elijah Stuart in the Georgian Symmetry style with Italianate features, segmental arched windows, double brackets under the eaves and quoining on the corners. The double-hung front door has a fanlight and the second floor door has a keystone arch linking the same colour detail line across the front of the house.

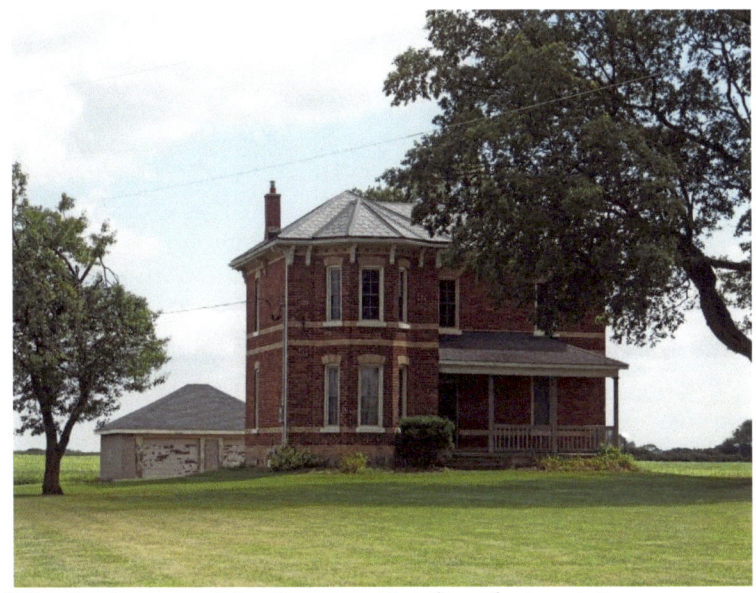

Maple Avenue North – cornice brackets, string courses, dichromatic brickwork, voussoirs above windows

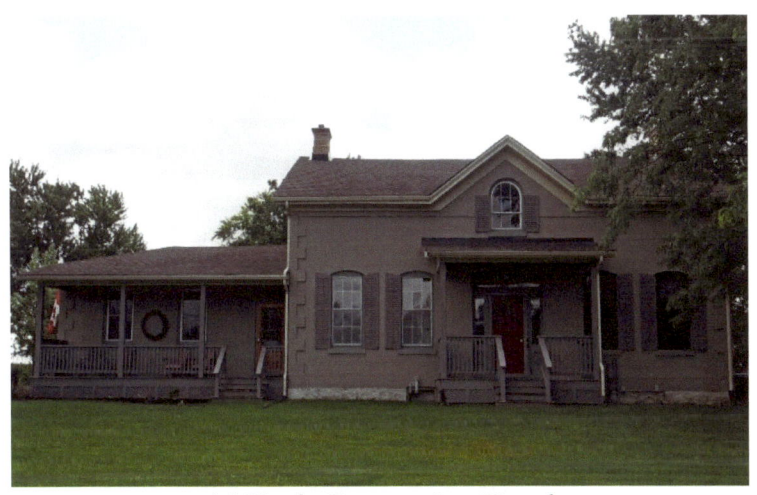

46 Sixth Concession Road

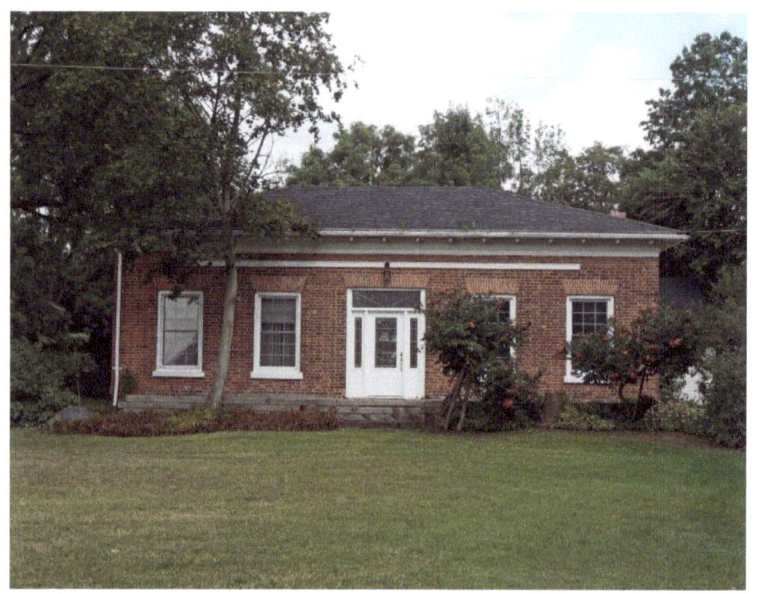

38 Sixth Concession Road – Windrush Farm circa 1850 – red-bricked Regency cottage

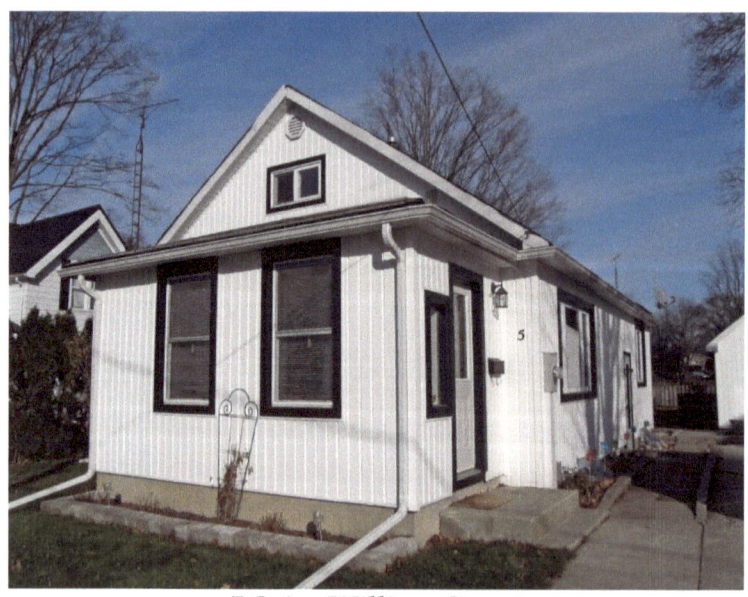

5 Saint William Street

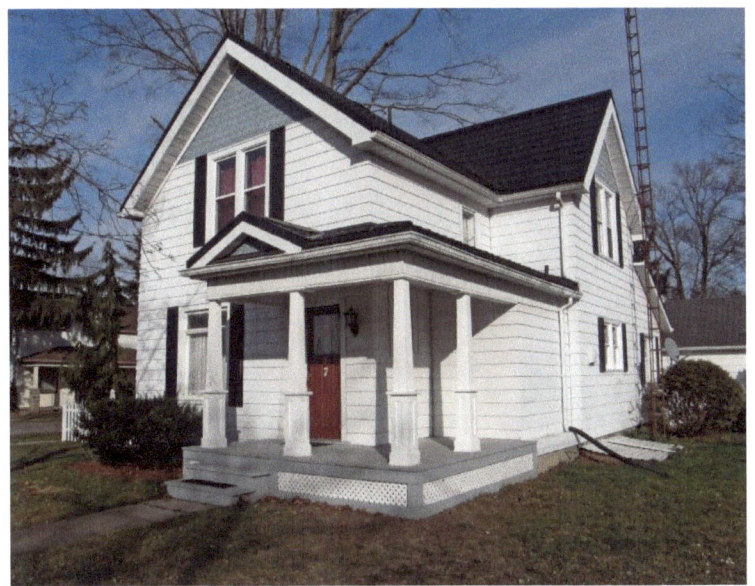

7 Saint William Street

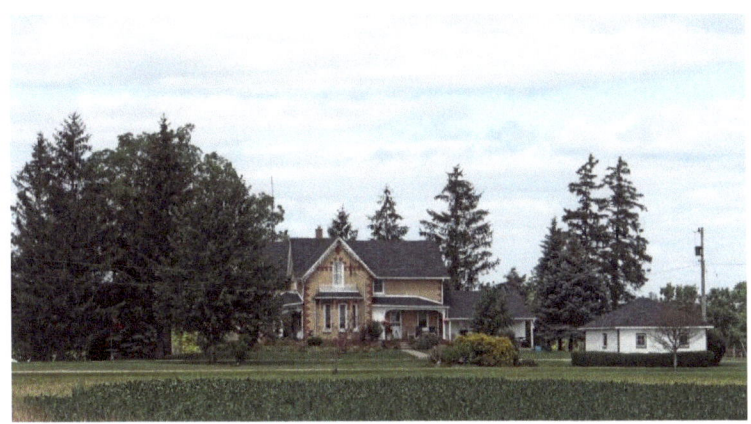

378 Seventh Concession Road – Ontario Farmhouse – verge board trim on gable, dichromatic brickwork, iron cresting around second floor balcony above bay window

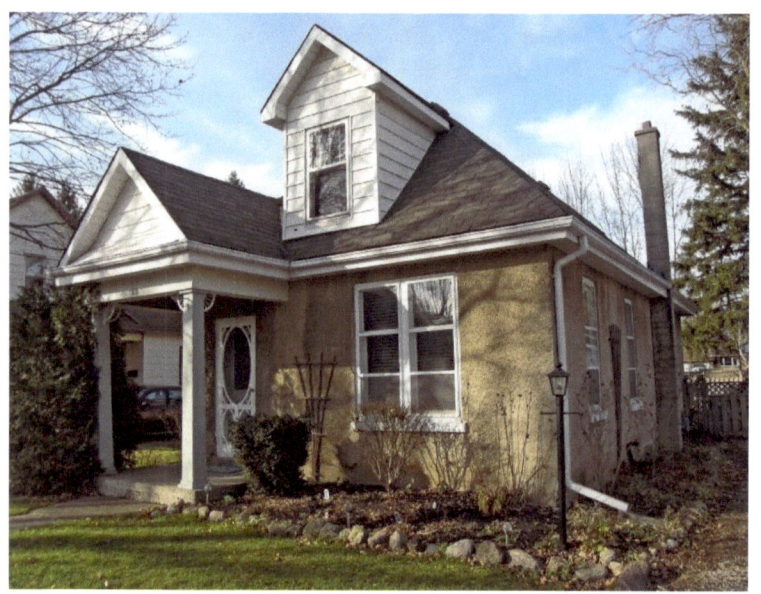

23 Dufferin Street – dormer, pediment

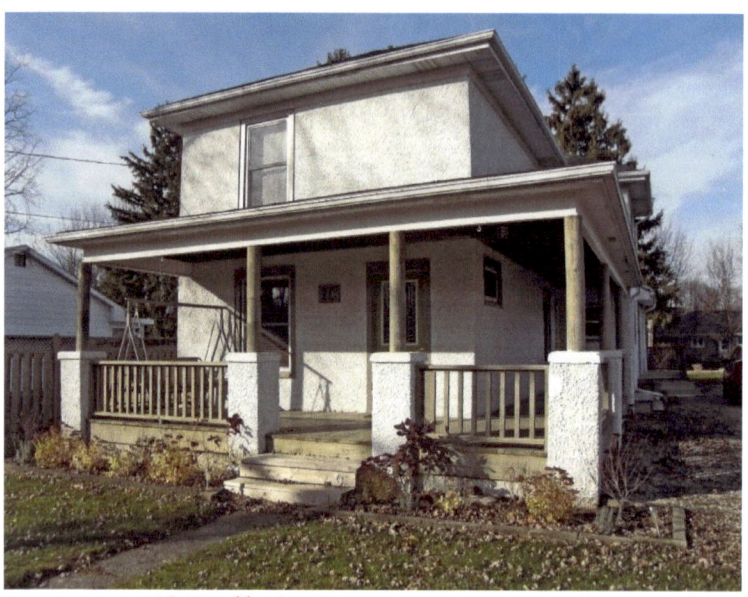

19 Dufferin Street – wraparound veranda

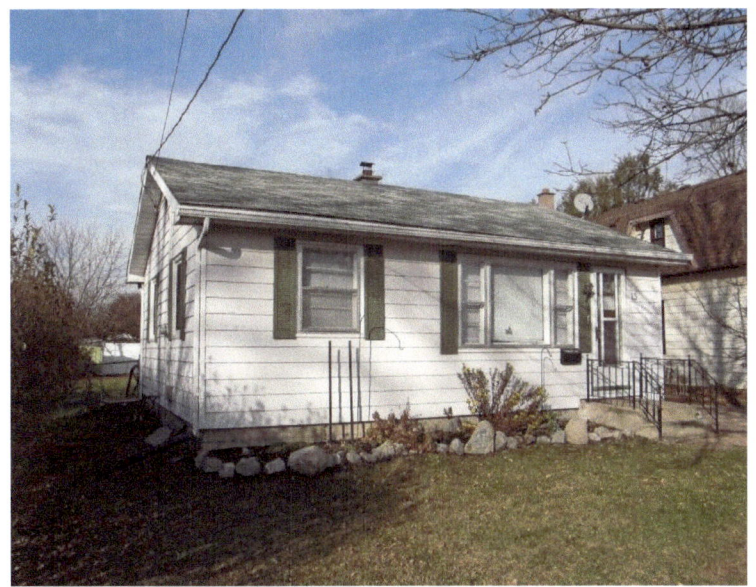
15 Dufferin Street

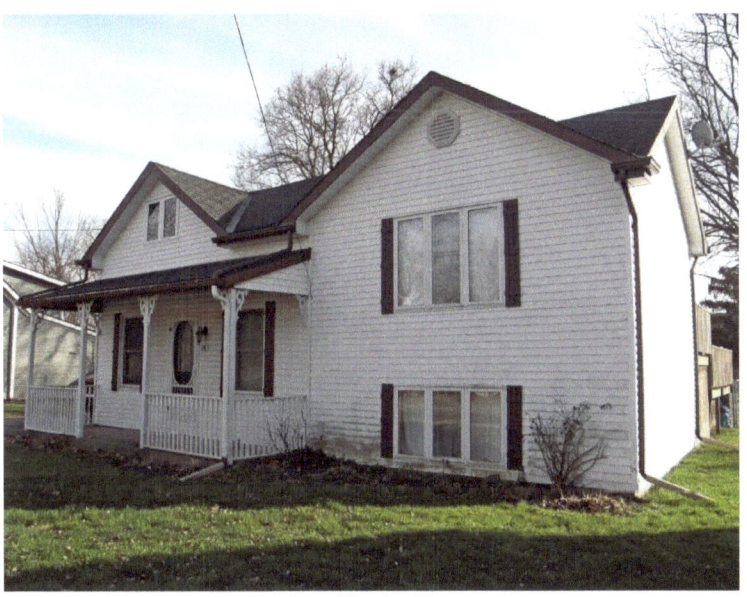
14 Dufferin Street

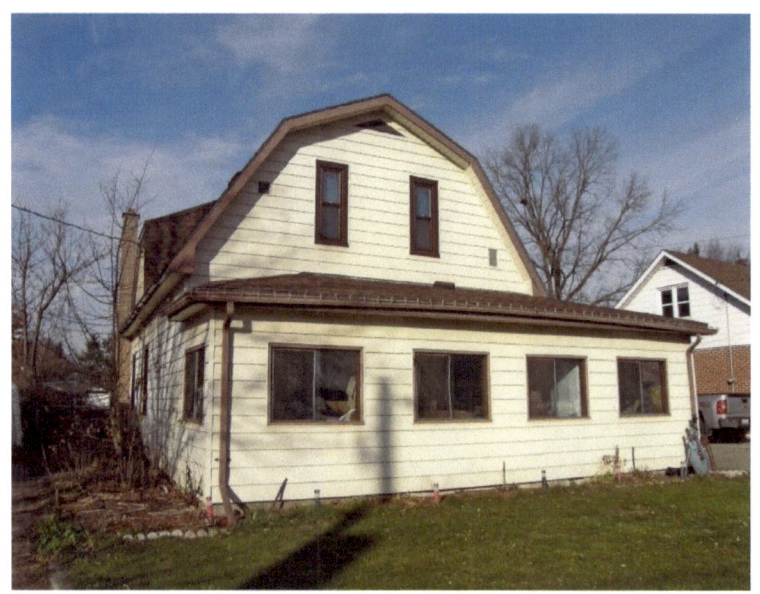

13 Dufferin Street – Neo-colonial – gambrel roof

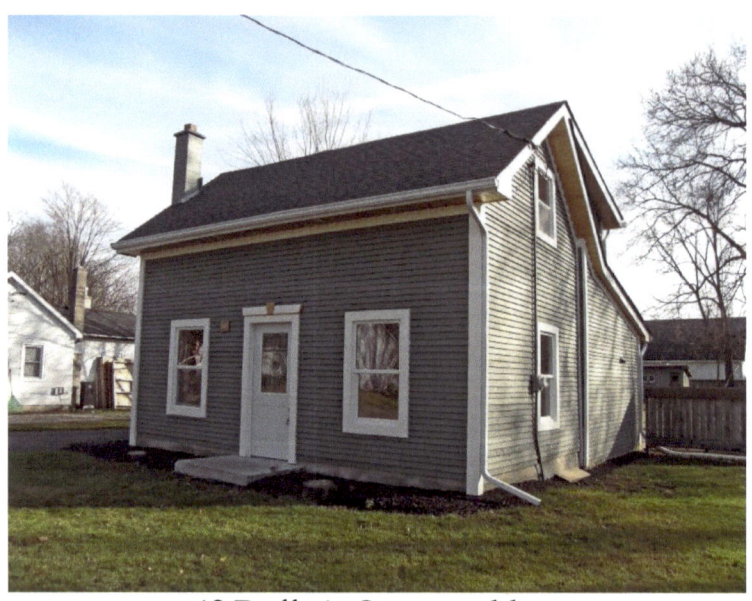

12 Dufferin Street - saltbox

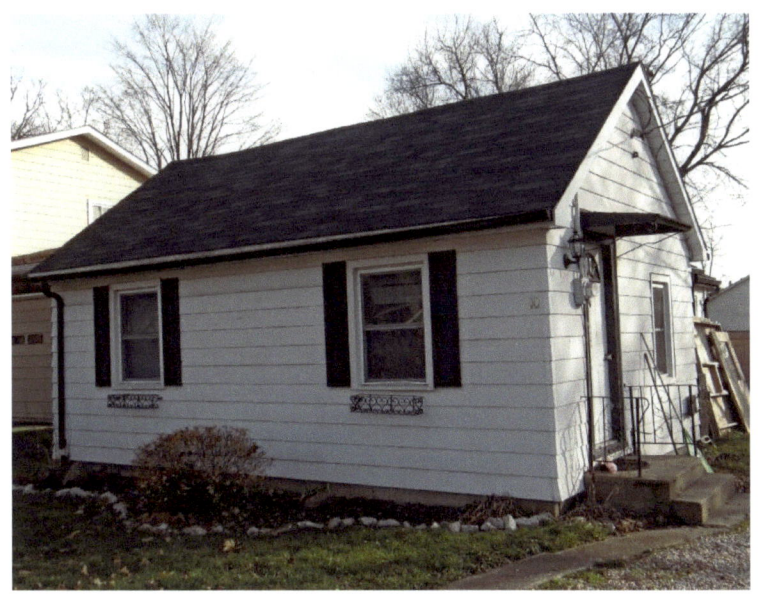

10 Dufferin Street

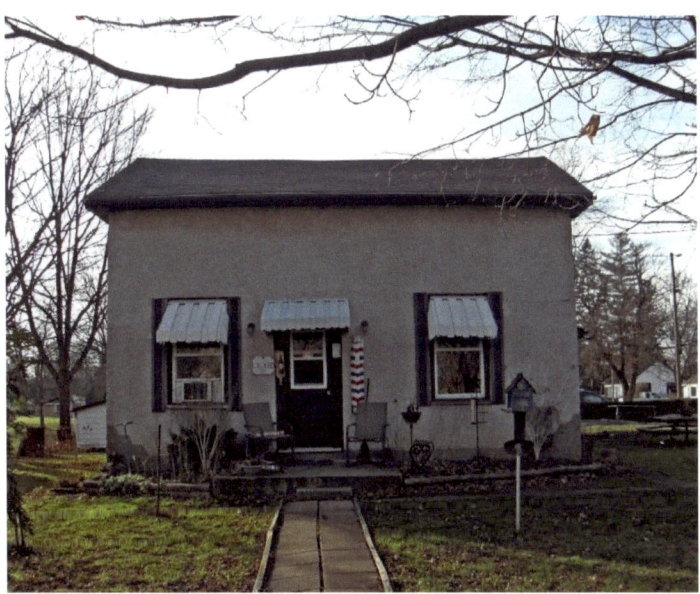

5 Jarvis Street

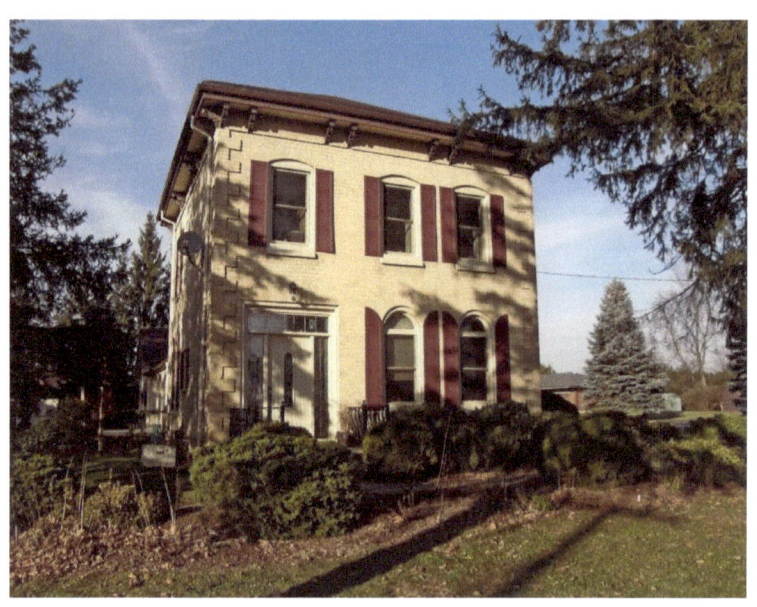

2 John Street – Heritage Property – 1870 – Italianate, hipped roof, cornice brackets, corner quoins, sidelights and transom, bric-a-brac on veranda

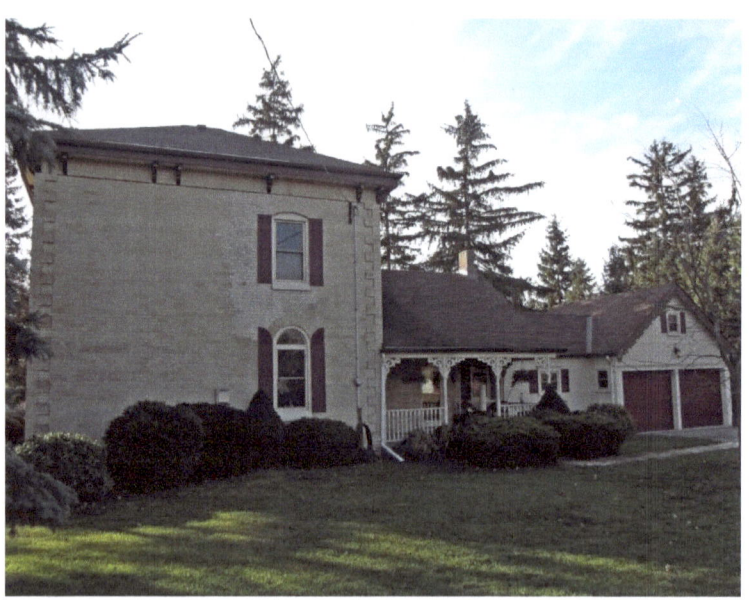

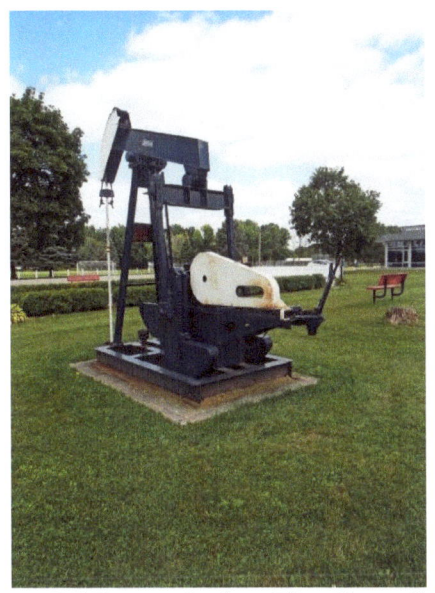

14 Potter Drive – Oil Pump Jack – The first oil well in Gobles was drilled by Austin Smythe in late 1959. There were about sixty oil wells drilled. In 2001 this pump jack was restored by the Burford Historical Society and placed on a cement pad in front of the Burford Community Centre.

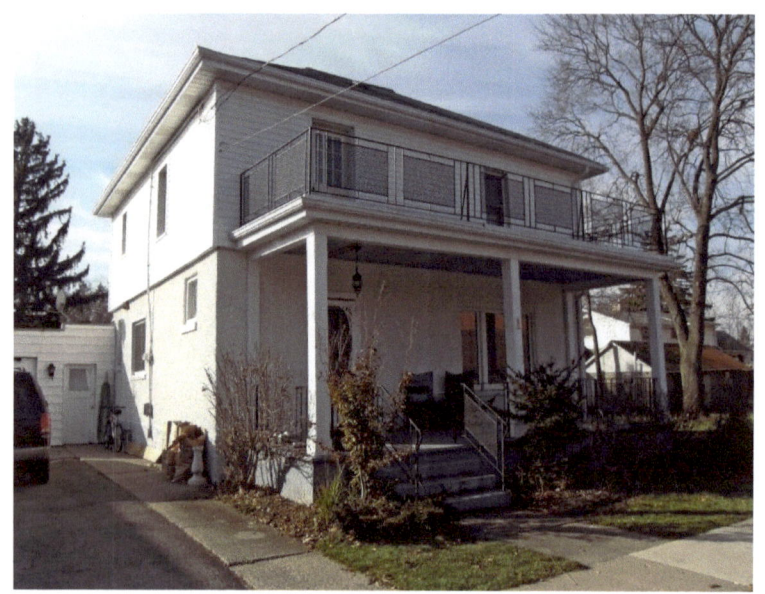

1 Alexander Street

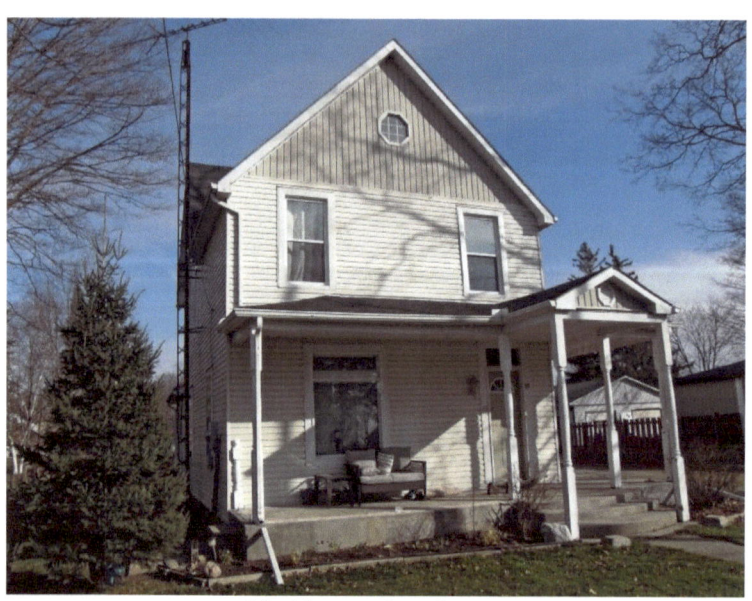

10 Alexander Street

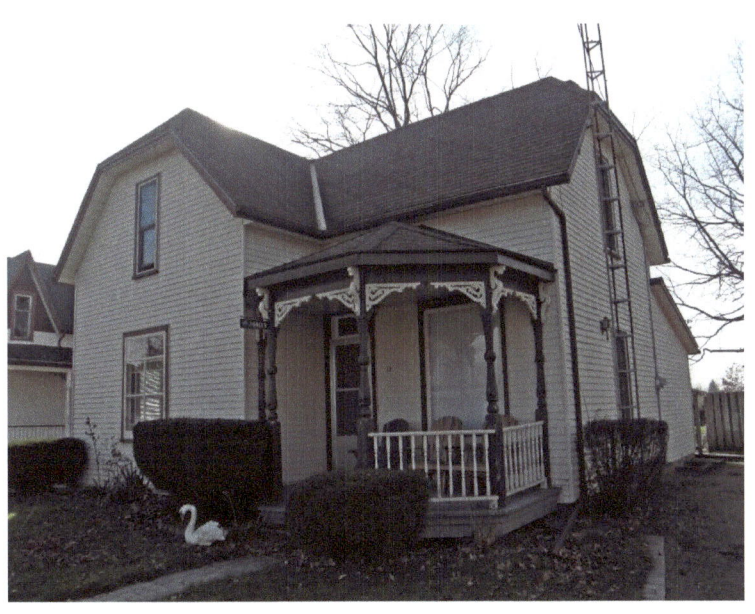

13 Alexander Street – chipped gables, bric-a-brac on porch

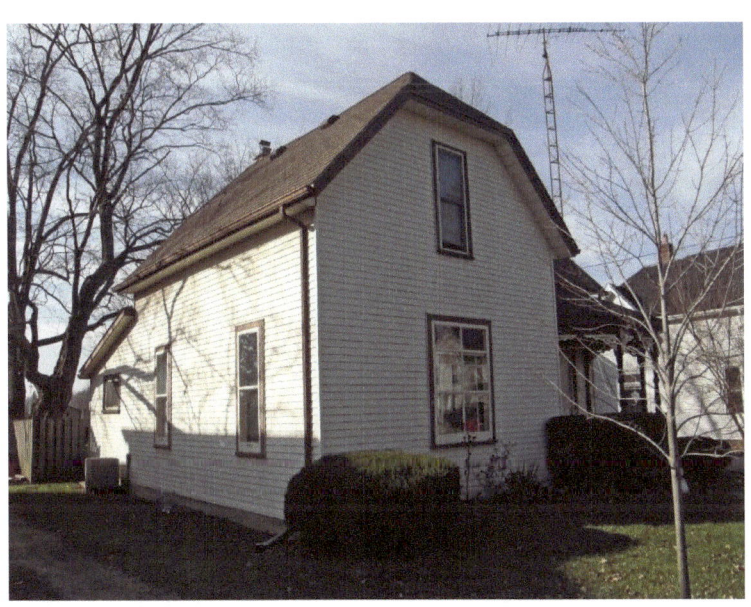

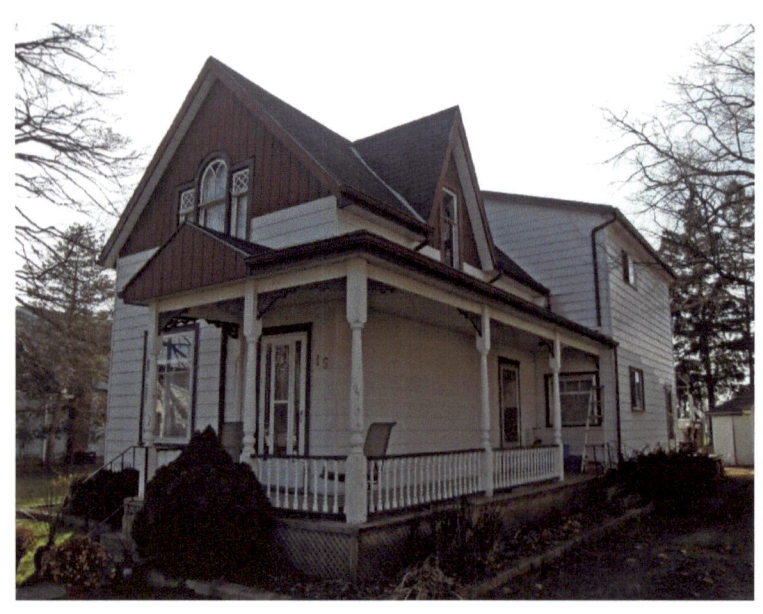

15 Alexander Street – Palladian window, turned wooden porch supports

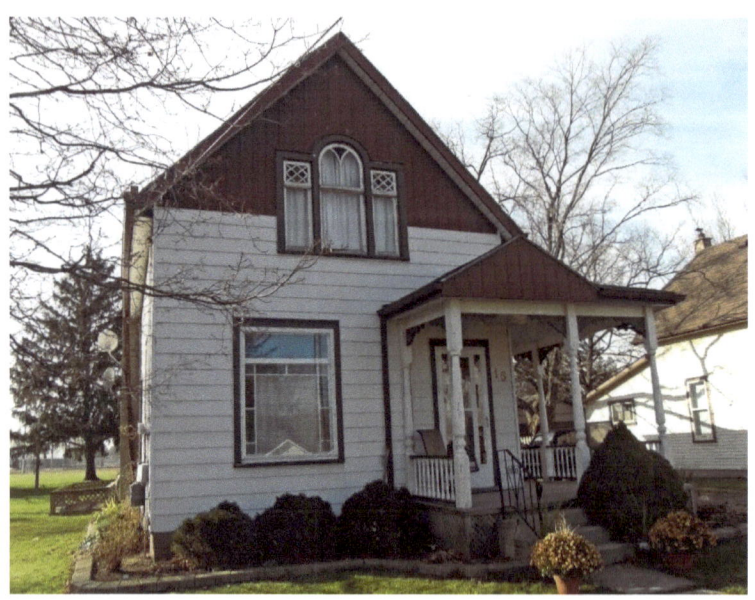

Architectural Terms

Bay Window: A window that projects out from a wall, in a semicircular, rectangular, or polygonal design. Used frequently in Gothic and Victorian designs. Example: 179 King Street, Page 45	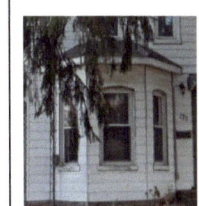
Brackets: a decorative or weight-bearing structural element which forms a right angle with one side against a wall and the other under a projecting surface such as an eave or roof. Example: 146 King Street, Page 34	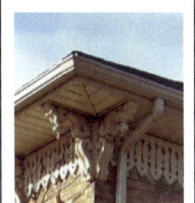
Capital: The uppermost finish or decoration on a column. A Doric column is characterized by a plain column with no base, a shaft with twenty flutings, and a simple capital with a simple entablature. Example: 155 King Street, Page 38	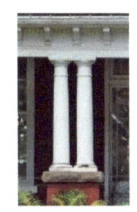
Dichromatic brickwork: the use of two colours of brick, tile or slate to decorate a façade. Example: Highway 53, Page 9	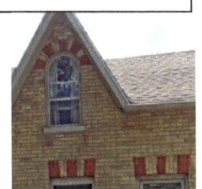
Dormer: (French for "sleep") a gable end window that pierces through the plane of a sloping roof surface to create usable space in the top floor or attic of a building by adding headroom. Example: 154 King Street, Page 37	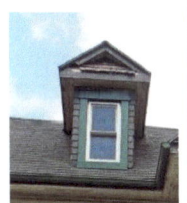

Gable: the triangular portion of a wall between the edges of a sloping roof. Example: 378 West Quarter Townline Road, Page 11	
Gambrel Roof: a symmetrical two-sided roof with two slopes on each side; the upper slope is positioned at a shallow angle, while the lower slope is steep. It is similar to a mansard roof, but a gambrel has vertical gable ends instead of being hipped at the four corners of the building. Example: 175 King Street, Page 44	
Hipped Roof: a roof where all sides slope downwards to the walls with no gables. Example: 49 King Street, Page 17	
Iron Cresting: A decorative ornament along the top of a roof. Iron cresting was popular in the Baroque era and also in Italianate, Victorian, Second Empire and Queen Anne styles of architecture. Example: 161 King Street, Page 41	
Keystones and Voussoirs: a voussoir is a wedge-shaped element used in building an arch. A keystone is the central stone that locks all the stones into position, allowing the arch to bear weight. A keystone is often enlarged and embellished. Example: 55 Maple Avenue North, Page 48	

Lancet Window: a tall, narrow window with a pointed arch at its top. Example: 104 King Street, Page 25	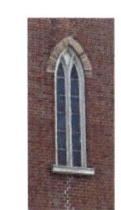
Palladian Window: a large window that is divided into three sections with the centre section larger than the two side sections and usually arched. Example: 15 Alexander Street, Page 60	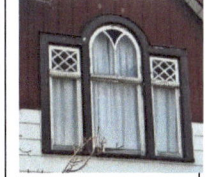
Pediment: a triangular section above the door or portico, usually supported by columns. The inside of the triangle is called the tympanum. Example: 90 King Street, Page 22	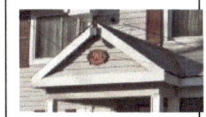
Quoin: masonry blocks at the corner of a wall, often a decorative feature, usually larger or of a different colour than the rest of the wall. Example: 280 Maple Avenue South, Page 7	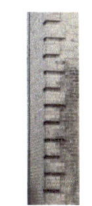
Sidelight: a vertical window that flanks a door, and is often used to emphasize the importance of a primary entrance. **Transom Window:** the light above the doorway, also called a fanlight. Example: 49 King Street, Page 17	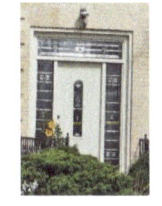

Tower: A circular, square, or octagonal vertical structure higher than the surrounding structure that is usually part of an existing building and is created either for extra defense or for a specific purpose such as a clock or a bell tower. Example: 126 King Street, Page 28	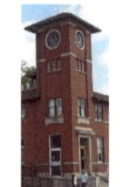
Verge board and Finial: also called bargeboards – hang from the projecting end of a roof and are often elaborately carved and ornamented. **Finial:** ornament added to the top of a gable, pinnacle, canopy or spire – a Gothic element. Example: 161 King Street, Page 41	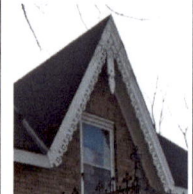

Building Styles

Edwardian, 1900-1930 – This style bridges the ornate and elaborate styles of the Victorian era and the simplified styles of the 20th century. Edwardian Classicism provided simple, balanced facades, simple rooflines, dormer windows, large front porches, and smooth brick surfaces. Voussoirs and keystones are used sparingly and are understated. Finials and cresting are absent. Cornice brackets and braces are block-like and openings have flat arches or plain stone lintels. Example: 152 King Street, Page 36	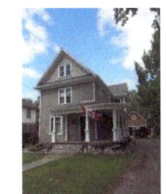
Georgian, before 1860 – This style began with the British King Georges in the 18th century. These buildings have balanced facades around a central door, medium-pitched gable roofs, and small paned windows. Example: 55 Maple Avenue North, Page 48	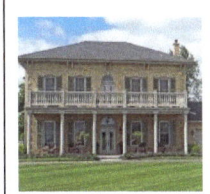
Gothic Revival, 1830-1890 – These decorative buildings have sharply-pitched gables with highly detailed verge boards, pointed-arch window openings, and dichromatic brickwork. It is a common style in Ontario. Example: 159 King Street, Page 40	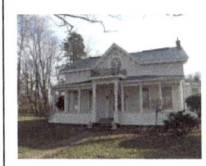

Italianate, 1850-1900 – A two story rectangular building with a mild hip roof, a projecting frontispiece, and generous eaves with ornate cornice brackets was the basis of the style; often there are large sash windows, quoins, ornate detailing on the windows, belvederes and wraparound verandahs. Italianate commercial buildings often have cast iron cresting and elegant window surrounds. Example: 306 Highway 53, Page 10	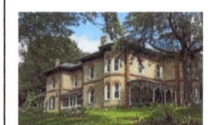
Ontario Cottage - one or one-and-a-half story buildings with a cottage or hip roof. The cottage roof is an equal hip roof where each hip extends to a point in the center of the roof. The hip roof has a long hip in the center. The Ontario Cottage is the vernacular design of the Regency Cottage which generally has a more ornate doorway and a partial or full verandah surrounding it. The roof can have a dormer, a belvedere, and generally two chimneys. Example: Highway 53, Page 8	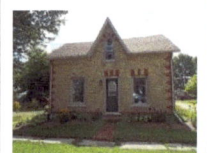
Queen Anne, 1885-1900 – This style is distinguished by an irregular outline featuring a combination of an offset tower, broad gables, projecting two-storey bays, verandahs, multi-sloped roofs, and tall, decorative chimneys. A mixture of brick and wood is common. Windows often have one large single-paned bottom sash and small panes in the upper sash. Example: 80 King Street, Page 19	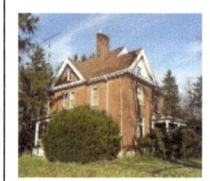

Regency, 1830-1860 – This style originated in England in 1815 and spread to Ontario later in the 19th century as British officers retired to Canada. It is a modest one-storey house with a low-pitched hip roof and has a symmetrical front façade. Example: 110 King Street, Page 26	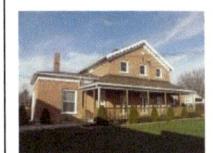
Saltbox: A saltbox is a building with a long, pitched roof that slopes down to the back, generally a wooden frame house. A saltbox has just one storey in the back and two stories in the front. The asymmetry of the unequal sides and the long, low rear roof line are the most distinctive features of a saltbox, which takes its name from its resemblance to a wooden lidded box in which salt was once kept. The earliest saltbox houses were created when a lean-to addition was added onto the rear of the original house extending the roof line sometimes to less than six feet from ground level. Example: 12 Dufferin Street, Page 54	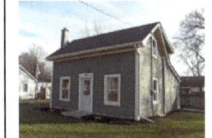
Tudor Revival – exposed timbers with stucco infill, multi-paned windows. Example: King Street, Page 30	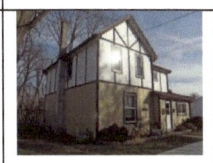
Vernacular/Traditional Mode 1638 - 1950 Influenced but not defined by a particular style, vernacular buildings are made from easily available materials and exhibit local design characteristics. Example: 89 King Street, Page 21	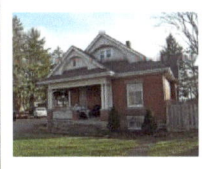

www.ingramcontent.com/pod-product-compliance
Lightning Source LLC
Chambersburg PA
CBHW040233220526
45473CB00001B/230